Ghost Girl

Also known as the School Janitor

By

Danny McKinney

Copyright © 2022 by Danny McKinney - All Rights Reserved.

It is not legal to reproduce, duplicate, or transmit any part of this document in either electronic means or printed format. Recording of this publication is strictly prohibited.

All scripture references are from the King James Bible, which is in the public domain.

Dedication

I dedicate this book to those who are working hard to write and publish the books placed on their hearts and those who encourage them to stay the course and get it done.

Acknowledgment

Bill Harris is a friend who just kept challenging me to write and encouraging me to share the stories from my past and in my heart. He is a good man, and I am happy to give Bill a shout-out. "Hey, Bill! We did it at last!"

About the Author

Danny McKinney is a retired minister and language arts middle school teacher. He, along with his wife and three children, spent the bulk of their working years in New Mexico, where they developed a love for the people and its culture. This is his second book.

Table of Contents

Dedication ii

Acknowledgment iii

About the Author iv

Chapter 1 1

Chapter 2 11

Chapter 3 28

Chapter 4 35

Chapter 5 41

Chapter 6 47

Chapter 7 57

Chapter 8 74

Chapter 9 88

Chapter 10 105

Chapter 11 125

Chapter 12 133

Chapter 13 144

Chapter 14 149

Chapter 15 166

Chapter 16 174

Chapter 17 198

Chapter 18	214
Chapter 19	234
Chapter 20	239
Chapter 21	254
Epilogue	279

Chapter 1

I want you to know right from the start that I am just a school janitor. I know lots of people like to call us custodians, but really, a janitor will do it. I work over at the middle school. It's been there for half of forever. There are some framed pictures in the front office that show the grounds before the building was built. Most of the roads and houses and businesses that I see every day driving in weren't even there when they built this place. To be honest, this school is sort of the ghetto for middle school these days. When some poor kid is asked where he goes to school and has to tell, he'll say something like, "You know, the school over by the park off of Idaho." If he's lucky, they won't know their city geography very well and will just kind of nod and change the subject. If, however, they know the place, they always give this knowing look, and if they are a kind-hearted person, then they change the subject. However, the socially incompetent will go on about how they've heard that school doesn't have very much technology, or that all the desks are super old and isn't that the place where they caught that kid with drugs, and don't they have gangs there, and on and on. The clincher is, "I heard that school was haunted. Didn't a little girl get killed there? Now she haunts the halls of Patton Middle? Isn't that true? Well, at least that's what I've heard."

For folks who have been in town for years, they know the story of the little girl who was killed at our school, long before I came there, when one of the janitors closed up the bleachers after a basketball game, only to hear the screams of a twelve-year-old girl who had crawled back there and hid. She may have been reading a book. You know how you can really get into the storyline, and then the next thing you know, you are just lost in it, and everything else just disappears. Reading Stephen King's 11.22.63 or John Grisham's A Painted House did that to me. And Peter Heller's book, Dog Stars, did you read that one? I loved that book. I never wanted it to end. Well, anyway, a janitor that reads, right? Who knew? Back to this little girl, it may even be that she had fallen asleep because the gym was empty, and surely, she would have realized that and gotten out of there and caught up with her family if she weren't either envisioning a story or dreaming of one.

When the janitor reversed the bleachers after he heard the screams, he rushed under on the home side and found this little girl, she couldn't have weighed more than eighty pounds, her long dark hair had a tint of strawberry in it (or was it so dark it was almost blue?) and it was caught in the front wheel of the bleachers. She looked at him as the light faded from her almost golden eyes. He rushed back and reversed the powered bleachers. When he came back to the girl, he found…you know, when I tell this story, it gets very gruesome. I hate that. Facts are facts, I agree, but sometimes all the details don't need to get out to get the story across. I came to that hard reality when a little four-year-old girl came to me once and told me that she had heard that I had a ghost story. She had heard from some source or other the story that I am telling you now. Crazy how a story can own you rather than what seems to be the other way around. I wanted to tell her the story but knew that it was way too grotesque in its inception to tell it graphically. So, I adjusted it greatly. It still said the same thing; it just needed a buffer for those who either can't deal with the harsh rawness of the story or who would just rather skip it, thank you very much. Maybe they have had enough hard reality that makes them opt out of any more unnecessary doses of it. Fair enough. With that in mind, here is what I told the little girl as I came to where we are now in the story.

Do you remember the story of Jesus and how he was crucified for our sins? Do you remember how terrible that was, that people took the best man who ever lived and killed him on purpose? Now we know that God raised him up again three days later, but that didn't take away from the awfulness of the scene. Well, in this story, something really terrible happened too, but in this story, it was not on purpose. It was a really terrible accident. So, I will just say that the little girl got caught behind the powered bleachers by mistake when the janitor was cleaning up, he closed them, and the little girl got caught behind them and died. He felt really terrible about it, but he couldn't fix it. So, this is the story of another janitor that came along many years later who helped fix the problem and make an awful, horrible story come out good in the end. How was that? I mean, what would you have done? Fair warning: the next few pages contain the details. If you don't want to read it, skip to chapter three. Easy.

As I was saying earlier, he saw that her skull had been crushed. Even though I wasn't there, the scene just gives me the willies, you know? Why do such things have to happen to children? She didn't have a chance. Her blood seeped out slowly onto the gym floor and onto the janitor's laced work boots. Well, honestly, I guess I read a lot of books, and that's the way I envision it. I know, call me crazy. The way I imagine it, the janitor then quickly worked to free her hair from the wheel. It had tangled itself two or three turns. He wrestled with it but then took out his pocket knife and cut the locks away. Throwing his knife down, he took the girl up into his arms and hustled out from under the bleachers, calling out to the empty gym. "Somebody, anybody, help! A girl's been…." He trailed off with a heavy sigh. "O my God! God, what can I do? O no! O no! O no!" He called out in exasperation. "This little thing. This poor thing. O my, O my. O God, what am I going to do?" Everyone else had gone home. There was no one there to help. No one to tell him what to do. He carried her limp body up to the front office, dripping blood all the way. It gives me the chills just thinking about it. The office was the only place in the school that had a phone. Remember, this is the 1960s. He put her limp body on the office floor and picked up the phone. This was long before the 911 system had been put in place. He didn't know the number for the police; he couldn't remember the number for the principal's house, so he called the only number that would come to his mind at the time. His own. After six agonizing rings, his wife answered the phone. Her voice was groggy as if she had been asleep.

"Hello?" She asked questioningly. It was way past polite hours for calling, and her husband never called from work. He just came in when he finished cleaning up after a game like he always had.

"Juanita, honey!" His voice was all a tither, and she knew something must be seriously wrong.

"What is it, Lee? What's the matter?" She responded back.

"Honey! O, Honey, I need you to call the ambulance. There's a little girl here that got caught in behind the bleachers. Honey, I'm afraid I've killed her!" His voice broke. A man brought up in the country, he wasn't one to cry, but he did not know what to do.

"O, No! O, No! Lee, baby, what happened?" She cried back, now fully awake.

"Juanita, honey, I don't know. I don't know, and I don't know what to do. Honey, I think I've killed her. What am I going to do?" He sobbed aloud. It was the first time she ever remembered him crying, and it broke her heart. She longed to take him in her arms and comfort him, but she could not. The phone and phone line stood between them. He had never broken, even when he lost his job with the county and was out of work for months, even when news came that his brother had been killed in some freak accident in the army.

Lee was strong and true, and… She gathered herself and knew he needed her right then, maybe more than ever. "Wait, Honey. It's okay. I'm sure it was an accident. I'm calling right now. You stay there. I'm getting off now so I can make this call. It's going to be okay. Uh, after I make this call to the hospital, I will call my friend, Pearl. I know it's late, but I think she can bring me down there. I'll be there soon. Honey, it's going to be okay. I love you, babe. It'll be alright. We're going to get through this," she said, trying to comfort him. He was sobbing openly now.

She heard his heartbreak, and it tore her up inside. She ended the conversation abruptly; with his crying, he couldn't possibly hear her anyway, and she was now sobbing herself.

"Bye, Honey," she said and hung up the phone. For a moment, she stared at it, then she shook herself and set the tumblers into motion. She picked up the phone book and quickly flipped through with trembling fingers until she found the hospital.

"Memorial Hospital front desk, can I help you?" Came a voice.

"There's been an accident at the junior high down by Wilson Park. A little girl's been hurt. Please, hurry. Please, hurry." His wife could hardly breathe.

The lady at the hospital caught the sense of desperation. "Don't worry, ma'am. I just need to get a little information. Are you calling from La Plata?"

"Yes, ma'am. La Plata, where else would I be calling from? We need help now! Please! My husband is over there, and he…." The hospital front desk receptionist interrupted.

"It's alright, Miss. Now you are going to have to calm down for us to get this done right. We have people call in here from Deming and Hatch and every other little place around. Now I know it's La Plata. There are two junior highs in town. Are you referring to Patton Junior High or Sierra Junior High?" She asked.

"Patton, Patton Junior High. The one down by Wilson Park. You have to know the place. My husband is the evening janitor over there. He is there all alone with a little girl that got caught somehow behind the bleachers; she's hurt bad. Please, please send help!" Juanita said in exasperation.

"I'll have someone sent over right away. Just hold on while I make that call." The receptionist said.

Ignoring the last statement, the janitor's wife hung up. She was so distraught. She wrung her chapped hands absent-mindedly. Years of being a washerwoman, taking in laundry to help keep the bills paid, and to be able to send money home to help her mom back in the hills of east Tennessee. The hands didn't matter. Her momma…her momma. She'd have done anything to have helped her. She tried to get her to move out to New Mexico. It would have saved Daddy's life, she figured. He had such a hard time with all the humidity, and the doctor told him, "Why don't you move our west, Lloyd? It would do you good. Your health would be so much better out there."

"I'll not be going out there to the middle of the desert. I saw how they landed a rocket out there and claimed it to be the moon. It might as well have been, for all the good land like that is. I've seen pictures, doc. That's all I need of the desert; thank you just the same. I'll take my chances here." And he did and died less than six months later from pneumonia. And so, she'd helped her momma. Couldn't get her to move out here either. "I'll just stay here and be buried by your daddy. We have been together more'n fifty years. He wasn't the best to me, but a promise is a promise. When I'm laid down, I want to be laid down there beside him, the old cuss," her mother had said. And just this past February, she'd done just that, finally having a massive stroke at the age of eighty-five that left her helpless for three weeks before she died. "Momma. Sweet Momma. How I wish you were here now. I just don't know what to do, Momma," she called out to the walls that could be seen and the spirits she could not see but knew were there just the same. What could she do? What had happened? Her poor husband. Who would help them now? She got on the phone right quick and called her friend, Pearl. The phone rang and rang. Finally, on the eighth ring, Pearl picked up the phone.

"Hello."

"Hello, Pearl, this is Juanita. I'm sorry to call you so late. Pearl, something has happened down at the school, and I need to get down there. Is there any way you could drive me down to the school? I'd be glad to pay you for the gas." You can just hear the way she said that. But then Pearl came back on. "Why, Juanita, honey, I'd be glad to take you down to the school. You don't need to worry about paying me for the gas. I'll hop in the car and be right there."

That was the way with Pearl. She and her husband, Gerald, had moved here after he got out of the Army at Fort Bliss. He was able to get a job right off, and the lack of humidity helped both of their breathing. They were from Maggie Valley, over in western North Carolina, and once they met Lee and Juanita, they became fast friends. Their accents and experiences were much the same, and they relied on each other, especially when they were feeling homesick. They spent many Sundays together, going first to the little church of Christ down on Miranda Street and then playing

Rook or dominoes or crochet or bowling or something else. It didn't really matter so long as they were together.

Anyway, Pearl just grabbed her keys and jumped in the car, and off she went in a rush to get Juanita. Now think of this. She still had no idea what was the matter; she just knew that Juanita needed her, and so she sprang into action. That's what a real friend will do; I'll tell you that.

Chapter 2

The little girl was dead when the ambulance arrived. The janitor hung over them, the medical crew, fretting, crying out to them, to anyone who would look at him, "You've got to do something! Can't you give her a shot or something? She's just a little girl. She's just a little girl. It was an accident; I didn't know she was there. How was I supposed to know that someone had stayed behind? Everyone else was gone already. What was I supposed to do?" They looked at him, at first with pity and then irritation.

"Sir, you are going to have to stand back out of the way." A heavy man, with the name 'John' printed on his blue collared shirt, appeared to be in charge, though he looked very young.

"Will, take our friend here and calm him down. Get some information from him, anything. We just have to see if there is anything we can do." He said this, knowing as he did that this little girl's life was not coming back. Whatever happened, she was not in pain anymore. Still, there was protocol to follow, and there would be forms to complete explaining what they found and how they responded. It had to be right.

The young man, Will, took the janitor aside and asked, "So, what's your name?"

"Me? I'm, I'm," he had to think a minute. He was so distraught. "I'm a Lee, Lee Goodland. I, I, a, I'm the evening janitor here."

"All right, Mr. Goodland. I'm Will Cook. I work with John and Ab, over there, (Ab was thin as a rail and gawky, and it made Lee laugh when he saw John and Ab working together, despite himself.)

"Ahmmph." He wiped his nose on his blue sleeve and smiled at Will with tears in his eyes. "They kind of remind me of Laurel and Hardy," He said.

Will had heard this before, more than once, but the two worked so smoothly together that they were more like Batman and Robin. Heroes, as he saw them, though there didn't seem much they could do for this young girl now. She was long gone, he figured.

"It was all my fault," Lee said, breaking his train of thought. We just got those bleachers. "O yeah," everybody said. We sure would be top dog around here if we had those powered bleachers as they have at some of the schools in El Paso and Albuquerque. O Yeah. They kept talking about them, and I even got on board. It would be so great. After a hard day cleaning and then with a whole gymnasium floor to clean up, to just have this one little perk, bleachers, I didn't have to push in. What did it matter if I had to push them in? And now, look what has happened. It's my fault. I pushed the button like it was a prize or something. When she cried out, it was so pitiful. I thought, 'What is that?' She kept crying, sort of like a little puppy or something. Finally, I stopped the thing, and when I went over to the bleachers, she looked up at me. For the rest of my life, I will never forget how she looked up to me. Her eyes begged for something, but they didn't know what. I saw she was caught in the wheel. There was blood…I didn't know whether to reverse the bleachers or what, but I did. I reversed them, and then she cried out again, and I stopped the the…." He broke down again. Will reached over and patted his shoulder lightly to show that he was still there. He had handled some hard scenes, and this was definitely one of them. What made it worse was that this was not some scared little child or a worried mother but a man. A man that looked and sounded like a man until he broke. He was so pitiful then, and Will had no idea how to console him.

"I ran back over to the girl, and there she was, her long dark hair caught in the wheels of that thing. I tried to work it loose, but no dice. You know, Will, I saw she was fading. Maybe she was already gone, but I had to get her out of there. Her blood got on my boots and hands, but I couldn't think about that. I took out my pocket knife. I use it at work all the time, cutting open boxes and even sharpening pencils for the kids if they happen to need that done. Anyway, I took out my knife and started cutting away the hair. I hated to cut her long beautiful hair, but I didn't know what else to do. I had to get her out of there. I had to, Will." He cried uncontrollably again. Wiping his nose again on his now encrusted sleeve, he continued.

"Will, I got her out of there and ran her up to the school office. I knew I needed to call for help. We only have the office phone. Well, there might be, yes, there is another one back in the teacher's lounge, but I didn't think of that. So, I took her and ran up to the office. When I got there, I couldn't settle down to know how to call or who to call. I found the phonebook on top of the secretary's desk, but when I tried to find a number there to call, I couldn't even see the pages, my eyes were so full of tears. I don't cry, Will. You've got to believe me. I never cry. But I…Anyway, I grabbed the phone and called home. I didn't need to see those numbers to call them. My wife, Juanita, called for me. She said she was going to try and get her friend, Pearl, to bring her over here. I…" Will cut him off. John and Ab were waving to him. "Mr. Goodland, I am sorry, we have to go. We are going to get the girl over to the hospital now. Do you think you will be alright?" He asked as he was moved quickly back toward the ambulance.

"Me? O yeah, yeah, I'll be fine, Will. Thanks for everything," Lee murmured as he waved a trembling hand. He watched Will as he jumped into the back of the emergency vehicle, and just like that, the double doors were closed, and the ambulance lights were shining back at him in the night. He watched them go, red tail lights glowing as it drove quickly toward the hospital where she would be confirmed dead by the physician on night duty and then taken to the morgue. Her parents were yet to be notified because no one knew who she was. She couldn't have been more than twelve or thirteen, and her tiny body had nothing on it to identify her.

With the ambulance gone, the dark descended on Lee as he turned and looked back at the school and thought of the gymnasium just on the other side. For the longest time, he stared, not at the building itself but at what that school had been to him. He was the evening janitor. He just wanted to do his job and keep things in order. He was supposed to be one of those people that others know is there but really pay him little mind. He liked it that way. The janitor turned to go back inside the school, and then, without warning, he began to convulse in a wave of sobs and cries. *What had happened?* He just wanted to work a little longer and retire to a quiet life with his wife, and now, somehow, he had killed a little girl. It wasn't his fault. It wasn't his fault. It couldn't be his fault. He had shut those bleachers many times after games. Always pushing them in manually, and no kid had ever remained there long after the game when everyone had left. How could he have known? Then they put these powered bleachers in. They were great, and he was so proud. The school had stepped up, and he had stepped up. He had powered bleachers. Such a big shot, and now look at what had happened. He knew it wasn't his fault. It couldn't be his fault. How was he supposed to know? Then there was this voice. There was this voice. It started talking to him from somewhere. This voice. Was it inside his head, or did he hear things? He heard it again. It was the voice of a child. A girl. "Hey, mister. Hey mister, don't blame yourself for what happened. You didn't know I was back there. I just, well, my friend ditched me, and I didn't know what else to do. My parents were working, and I was supposed to hang out with my friend and even spend the night with her. But then, another girl we knew came along, and all of a sudden, they were playing and even making fun of me. They didn't want me around. I didn't want to let them see me cry, so I just left. I went over to the school, and the doors were still open. I guess there were still teachers working in there or something. I went inside and down the hall. The library was still open, so I went in and found this cool book my teacher was talking about today in Language Arts. It was called The House on Mango Street. It was about a girl, sort of like me; it turned out when I started reading it. I brought it back to the gym and was reading it under the bleachers when I guess I fell asleep. That's why I was there when you closed the bleachers. This wasn't your fault. Don't feel bad, Mr. Goodland." He couldn't believe he was hearing a dead girl talk to him. His reasoning faculties were all broken down now. He just knew that he had killed a little girl. A tiny little girl with long beautiful hair. She was just a little girl.

"I am so sorry. Are you, I mean, how am I talking to you?" He rubbed his hand through his thinning hair. "I just wanted to finish up for the night. I was all but done. But now look what I've done.

This is all my fault," he said, back to the voice, the ghost, the girl, whatever he was talking to. Then this other Voice, whether it was his conscience, or the devil, or what he did not know, but this other inner voice was also talking to him, shouting really. "You killed her. YOU killed her. What kind of man are you?"

He began to mumble and cry out, "No. No. No! It wasn't me! I didn't do it. It's not my fault! What could I have done? You heard what the girl said. She said it wasn't my fault. I didn't mean to," He cried back, but the Voice would not leave him alone. Shaken to his core, he turned away from the school building and walked to his truck. The old red Ford pickup sat there in the parking lot, out near the road, alone. Its paint was faded like its owner. Tired. Still working but used up. Like him. No one else was there. He quickened his pace as he neared the truck, trying to distance himself from the scene and the voices that wouldn't seem to leave him alone. Lee opened the truck door and looked inside. He couldn't get the voices in his head to stop accusing him on the one side and forgive him on the other. He knew it was not his fault, but he couldn't get past the idea that he had just taken a little girl's life. "Guilty!" his conscience cried. "No! He didn't mean it," the girl called back. "I wasn't even supposed to be there. It's okay, Mr. Goodland. I don't feel any pain now. I'm okay. I just need for you to be okay before I leave. I've been seeing some bright lights, and I can hear voices calling me. I know some of them. They are the voices of people that sound so familiar. I know it's my family that has gone on before, Mr. Goodland. I am excited to see them. I'm not afraid, Mr. Goodland. God knows the number of our days, Mr. Goodland. He's just calling me to join that great crowd of believers, of witnesses to his goodness, Mr. Goodland. I'm going to them, Mr. Goodland, but I need to know you are going to be okay." The girl's voice waned as the Voice, the one that was haunting him, maybe his conscience, he didn't know, kept up a rhythmic pounding in his head: "Guilty, guilty, guilty, guilty, guilty, guilty." He squeezed his head and shook it violently. All he knew for sure was that he needed to finish up cleaning the school. There was still work to do. He had never left a job undone. He was a man that could be counted on. He was responsible for the care of the school. He knew the right thing to do and was intent on doing it. Then he remembered that there was indeed more work that needed to be done. There was the cleaning up of the girl's blood. It was not only in the gym but streamed down the hall and on the office floor. They couldn't go into the school with a little girl's blood on the floor everywhere. "No!" He shouted out loud. "I can't! Not tonight," he said back to himself. He couldn't do it. Not tonight. Not ever. "You killed her," the Voice said. "No, I did not!" He shouted back. "Killed her. Go back in there and look at the blood. That girl's blood is on your hands, Lee Goodland. Get back in there and clean it up!" The Voice commanded.

The girl again. "It was not his fault! He didn't know I was back there! It was just an accident! It could have happened to anyone."

"It's like she said. It is not my fault!" Lee yelled back, shouted back at night. "I won't go back in there. I can't bear to see the blood. It's, no, no!" He struggled with finding the right words to answer himself. I won't do it. Not tonight and not ever!" and without locking the school or even closing the gym doors, he jumped up inside his truck, slamming the door, trying to close the haunting voices out. He started the old tired engine and revved it up. Where was he going? He couldn't go home. His wife hadn't shown up. Maybe she blamed him too. It was so terrible what had happened. Someone had to be to blame. Who else but him? He asked himself. "O, no!" He said. "I guess I know the Voice is right. This is totally on me. The little girl is too young to understand these things," he reasoned. "That's right. Now you are thinking straight. She doesn't get it, but you know? Someone has to bear the blame. Who else but you, Lee Goodland?" What would he do now? He didn't do it on purpose. He was as much a victim here as the little girl, but the Voice, his conscience, whatever it was, it wouldn't stop. Why wouldn't it stop? "Yeah, right. It was an accident. Well, sir, you have to be the one to tell her parents. You robbed them of their little girl. And no matter whether it was an accident, as you say or not, they are only going to see you as the man who killed their little girl. You, Lee Goodland. You have to live with that."

"No! No, you know it was an accident. It was a mistake."

"Yeah, O, yeah. A mistake. You just killed a little girl. Some mistake. But buddy row, it is a mistake that is going to face you for the rest of your life. Deal with it. You did it."

"No!" The little girl tried again. "You can't blame him for something I did. He was just doing his job. This is not his fault. It just happened." Then turning back to Lee, she said, "Mr. Goodland, this is not on you. Don't listen to it. It's got this all wrong."

"O no. No, this is on you, Lee. You know it. The little girl died too young to know what happens when something like this goes down. You know you can never work at the school again. Who will trust you? Everybody who sees you will whisper, "That's him. He's the janitor that killed that little girl. You know what I'm saying is true. The little girl is nice and all, but she didn't live long enough to know how the adult world works. She thought her friend was being cruel; if she only knew. Even your wife, at best, will just pity you. Your life is over!" And then the Voice or conscience or whatever it was turned and addressed the girl directly. "Baby girl, this man, whether he did it on purpose or not, just did you one big favor. He took you out before you found out how cruel life could be. Yeah, I'd say he did you a favor."

Lee called back. Shouted really. "No! She had the right to live. Everybody chooses their own path. Don't listen to him, girl, don't listen…." His voice trailed off. He was so confused. He felt lost. How could this have happened?

He put the truck in gear and, pulling out of the school parking lot, headed north on Interstate 25. The highway had been built only a few years earlier and was the fastest way north. The fastest way to anywhere but Patton Junior High. He had to get away. He couldn't think about his wife. She'd be better off without him. Maybe. He didn't know. He did know that, intentional or accidental; the girl was dead. He had just killed a girl. He couldn't think about his job. The day janitor would clean it up. He hated to leave it to him; it was wrong for him to leave it with him, but he couldn't; he just couldn't go back in there. He didn't know where he was going. That Voice, where had it come from? Why was it blaming him? He drove faster. He drove past the city lights. He drove out under the desert sky, which had grown stormy, and the winds had picked up, pushing his pickup to the east as he drove north. He heard the girl again as if her voice was on the wind. What was she saying? It didn't matter. He gunned the truck. The old red truck engine responded like it too had to do whatever it took to get away from that damning Voice and the little girl. He just drove. He'd figure this out, somehow. He just had to get to a quiet place, away from the death and the voices.

Headlights shown on the school building and flashed around back by the gymnasium. The two-toned red and white four-door 1962 Plymouth Belvedere flashed its headlights bright. Juanita and her friend, Pearl, stretched their necks and strained their eyes, looking for some sign of Lee. "Lee always parks his truck out here on the edge of the parking lot. He likes to give the teachers and administrators good parking spots. Now there's nothing. What's come of him, Pearl?"

"Juanita, I guess he left. Maybe he went down to the hospital or something."

"Dad gum it. What should we do now? I'm sure he gave us out of coming. It's been more'n an hour since he called. Bless his heart. O Pearl, I have never heard him like that. He was so distraught. My poor, poor Lee. He'd never do anybody wrong on purpose, and now look what has happened to him. I'm sure he's all to pieces."

"Well, now, Juanita. We'll go to the hospital and find him. He'll be alright once you are with him. I am so sorry it took so long to get here. I always put my keys on the hook there by the door, but for some reason, they weren't there tonight. I finally dumped my purse out, and there they were, lodged somehow in the bottom of my purse. If I hadn't heard them jingle when I shook my purse, I never would have found them. I sure don't remember dropping them in my purse and have no idea how they got lodged in there like that. But I sure am sorry it took so long for me to get to you." She looked over at her friend and saw the tears rolling down her cheeks and off her chin. "Baby, it's okay. I'm sure he's at the hospital. Hush now. We'll be there in a minute."

The ladies were quiet for the rest of the ride over to the hospital. As they pulled up in the lot, they saw an ambulance crew talking among themselves as they walked away from the hospital out toward their cars, probably finished with their shift.

Pearl cranked down her window and called out: "Hey, have you folks just brought a little girl into the hospital? We are looking for the janitor that was there at the school."

The men looked back and forth toward one another. Then the big guy, who had 'John' over his breast pocket, stepped forward. "Um, ma'am, there was a janitor there at the scene when we left. I think he said his name was Lee. He was very upset. Will here talked to him for a while to calm him down. We had to go to get the little girl here to the hospital, but he was still there when we left."

"Uh, which one's, which one's Will?" Juanita said, leaning forward, wiping tears from her eyes.

A thin young man stepped forward. "Ma'am, I'm Will. I talked to Mr. Goodland. He was pretty stressed out when I talked to him, but he had calmed down some when we left. He told me he would be alright. We had to go, ma'am, or I wouldn't have left him until someone else got there. I think he told me he had talked to you, and you were going to be coming."

"Well, well," Juanita started and then burst out crying again. "We just don't know where he is and..." her voice trailed off. Pearl broke in.

"We went down by the school to meet him, but he was gone. We had hoped he might have followed the ambulance to the hospital. Will, did he say anything about going somewhere?"

"No, ma'am. Not that I recall. I'm really sorry. Maybe he went home or something. I guess I'd check there."

"Thank you, fellows. We appreciate it. Is, uh, is the girl going to be alright?" Pearl asked.

The men looked at one another, and John said, "Uh, ma'am, we are not supposed to talk about that kind of thing to non-family members. We turned her into the staff here. If they can help her, they will." He turned his eyes down as he said this. The women searched the young men's faces and then said, together, "Thank you, fellows. Thanks for what you do." And then the two-toned Plymouth drove out of the parking lot and headed back quickly to Lee and Juanita's house.

"He's there. I'm sure he's there. Of course, he is. I should have thought of that. We better hurry, Pearl. My Lee is there all by himself. He needs me. O hurry, Pearl, hurry." Juanita's words came out almost in a monotone. She was in some kind of automatic pilot now. It was the only way she could hold herself together. Pearl glanced at her friend and then set to getting to the Goodland house as quickly as possible. She sure hoped her friend's husband was there or, well, he was there. He had to be. As the car turned into the gravel drive, there was no sign of Lee's red Ford Pickup truck. Pearl shut the engine off, and Juanita jumped out of the car and raced into the house. The door was unlocked; they always left it unlocked, but it was closed, and everything was just as she had left it. There was no sign that Lee had been there. Juanita stepped back out on the porch and saw Pearl, just getting out of the car, making her way toward her.

"Any sign of him, Juanita?"

"No. No sign at all. Pearl, what's come of him? Do you reckon he might have gone to your house?"

"I'm not sure, honey, but let's drive over there and see."

Both women held their breath as they drove across to Pearl's house. Pearl lived alone mostly. Her husband, Gerald, was gone through the week driving a transfer truck. He drove for an oil company out of Artesia. He made good money driving, but he had essentially made his wife a weekday widow. The only thing that saved Pearl from going nuts about it was her friendship with Juanita. She loved Juanita and considered her more of a sister than a friend. The two were very close and would do anything for each other. A friendship like theirs was rare and precious. You don't get more than a handful of chances to come across a friendship like theirs in a lifetime, and these women were wise enough to know it.

As they came into the yard, they saw that Pearl's driveway was empty also. Gerald owned a 1960 Ford F-100, two-toned red and white, like his wife Pearl's Plymouth. People said it was cute how they had vehicles that were the same color. Gerald said when he saw his truck sitting over in the oil field where he picked up his truck which transported oil from the field to the refinery, it reminded him of his Pearl back home, and that put purpose behind his work. He worked for the Illinois Camp; I think they called it, and had asked Lee several times if he might be interested in a job transporting oil. There wasn't anything to it, he told Lee, and the money was good. There was no denying that, but Lee wouldn't give it a second thought. He and Juanita would make it somehow, and even working late as he did, at least he got to see her every day. There are just some things that money can't buy.

Pearl parked the car, and both of the ladies sat quietly for a time. Finally, Pearl said, "Juanita, honey, I want you to stay here with me tonight. There's no need for you to go back to that empty house alone. You can take the guest room. It will be nice to have company for a change."

Juanita sighed. "Thank you, Pearl, and I hate to put you out, but if you don't mind taking me home, I'd appreciate it. There's no telling where Lee is, but he might come home, and I need to be there when he does."

Well, Pearl took her home. Still no Lee. No sign that he had been there. Juanita thanked her friend and went inside to begin her wait and her prayers for her husband. By now, it was very late. The wind that had come up earlier had laid down, and all was quiet. Juanita walked into their bedroom and knelt down by the bed. "Lord, I don't know what has happened to Lee. Father, he has had a very bad thing happen to him tonight. You know that all too well. Please look after my man. God, I don't know what I would do without him. We don't always get along perfectly, but I love that man, Lord. Please let him know you are with him, and don't let him fall down further into despair. Show me what to do, Lord, and I'll do it. Till you do, I'll be right here, praying for Lee. Show yourself mighty, Lord, and bring my Lee home. I ask you this, humbly, and in Jesus' name."

Chapter 3

I know it's a crazy story. That was over fifty years ago. I didn't believe it. Any of it. You know how people talk, especially in a small town. Just a bunch of foolishness to keep them from being bored out of their minds or staying in someone else's business. I started working here at Patton in August of 2009. I had been working at Camino Real Middle School, but they moved me over here to take the head janitor job, and I've been here ever since. I guess I need to say that this town is growing. Camino was built in 1997, and, really, since the 1960s when Patton was built, four other middle schools have been built. The town population has grown from twenty-plus thousand to over one hundred thousand. All that said, this town still has that small-town feel. I don't know. Maybe I'm crazy. All this time, I have heard little stories every now and then of something weird happening that they were trying to pin on this ghost girl, but it was always with a wink, at least on my part. "Sure, okay," I'd say. You know how these old west towns are. Over in Mesilla, they have a ghost at the Double Eagle Restaurant, and then there's La Llorona and Billy the Kid and all that Jazz. There's a red-headed lady that haunts The Lodge up in Cloudcroft. All interesting and all nonsense, or so I thought. It wasn't until I came in early one Monday morning and saw Mr. McCrank scurrying up the hall that I began to wonder. Mr. McCrank was a retired Navy officer who, when you got to know him, was likable, sort of like an old grandpa. He always came off gruff and had a great evil eye, but it turned out, after several years of working under him, that he was just a guy after all. This is why his scurrying up the hall gave me pause. His breathing was a little ragged, and he put his hands on his knees when he looked up at me.

"Morning, Mr. McCrank." When he looked up, his face was pale, and I could tell that I had startled him. "Is everything okay, Mr. McCrank?"

He blustered a bit; then, he composed himself. It was just he and I in the school that early in the morning. "O, sure. Yeah. Hey, did you leave that radio on in Mrs. Montes' classroom last night?"

"Umm, No, sir. I did this wing of the school last. The teachers in this science hall tend to stay later than some of the others. I, a, vacuumed the floors and wiped down the boards and desks, picked up trash, like I always do, and hurried on down to Mr. Wilson's room. It must have been around six O' Clock by then…Why? What's going on down there? You look like you've seen a ghost," I said.

"No, no. It's just…well, when I came in, just ahead of you, I heard the radio playing down the hall. It was turned up super loud. Playing some old acid rock stuff. I never liked that back in the '70s, and I sure didn't want to be blasted out by it early on a Monday morning. I went down the hall and found the music was blasting out of Mrs. Montes' classroom. The door was locked, and

I had the darnedest time getting the thing open. Finally, I got the door open and, I don't know. It's crazy. The music had stopped. There was prickling in my skin; the arm hairs rose up like I had brushed my sock feet on the carpet. I went around looking for the radio. Finally, I found an old transistor radio, the battery kind, you know, lying over on a shelf. It wasn't even clicked on. I opened the back, and it didn't even have batteries in it! I looked around one last glance and got out of there. I had just closed the door and was headed back this way when you called my name." He wore a look on his face like it made him feel foolish for telling me, but also one of relief that he was able to unburden himself. "That's the craziest thing I've ever seen, Larry. That sound had to come from somewhere, but I don't know, the room itself seemed…."

"You want me to take a look, Mr. McCrank? There's surely some reasonable explanation for it."

"Yeah, do you have time? It'll only take a minute. I was in too big of a rush like I always am. You're sure to spot it right away," he said. We walked back to Mrs. Montes' room. The door was partially open. I took the knob and pushed the door the rest of the way. The creak of the door sent shivers down my spine. Now I was getting spooked. I reached to turn on the light and got an electrical shock. Pow! You know, just like when you are rubbing your sock feet on the carpet and then absent-mindedly turn on a light switch. I shook my finger. The hairs on my arm were all standing up. Mr. McCrank jumped back like he had been shot! We both gave each other a knowing look before continuing into the room. There was no radio playing, but there was a presence in the room. That's the only way I know to describe it. Just like that, we both pushed our way back out into the hall. Breathing heavily and then, a bit abashed, we looked at each other, surprise on our faces, and then let out a nervous laugh.

"Crap, Larry. What do you make of that?" Mr. McCrank asked.

"I, Huh, I huh, I, I, I don't know, Mr. McCrank. There is something off in that room. It felt so weird, like there was something else in there besides us. I know we have it all wrong, but that's what it felt like," I said, my eyes wide, mirroring his.

"I know I closed that door. Just now, before you said, 'Good morning.' And did you feel that?" He looked at me, expecting an answer. Now, as I said, I didn't believe those stories of the little girl and the school janitor who caused her death, or at least felt like he was the cause, as it is said around here. I didn't know whether he had lost his mind and offed himself. In fact, now that I think about it, I don't think I ever heard what became of that evening janitor, but there was something mysterious about it. That didn't have anything to do with me, and I couldn't see how talking about it would do anything but make a person look silly. Besides, all that had been years ago. That's what I had thought up till now, but something just happened in that room that wasn't way back then. Something just happened. Now. And it scared me good.

"I don't know, Mr. McCrank. I don't know. Something strange is going on in there. It might just be an overload of electricity running to that room somehow. I'll go check the breakers," I said, knowing in my heart that my spoken theory had no merit. Breaker. Right…

"Yeah, umm, I'll go with you," Mr. McCrank said as he caught up with me. We walked in silence down the hall, turning the corner and then walking all the way down the next hall and then turned again to go into the small room where the electrical shutoffs for all the classrooms were kept. The shiny tiles on the floor watched us as we scurried along. Neither of us said a word. The key slid into the lock easily enough, and we entered the school electrical power center. The cabinet was clipped shut. We opened the gray metal box and checked out the circuits. The door panel had each room labeled.

"Everything looks normal, Mr. McCrank. No smoke or anything," I said with a little laugh. Weird things just happen, I guess. Why, just the other day I…." My voice trailed off, and I put my hand up on the switchboard. The breaker for room 109 was tripped. I checked the door panel again.

"I don't know, Mr. McCrank. Can you take a look at this?" I stepped back so he could get a good look at the electrical box.

"What is it? Let's see. Mrs. Montes' classroom is down the first hall as you come in that front door, just down from the office. Her room is in the one hundred wing, then. Mrs. Martinez, room 101, Mrs. Saldonez, room 103, Ms. Walberg, room 105, Mr. Wilson, room 107, and Mrs. Montes, room 109...." His voice trailed off. "The breaker is tripped. What's going on here?" He exclaimed.

"I'm not sure, Mr. McCrank. Switch it back on and see if it trips again." He looked at me like I was crazy, but then he reluctantly reached up and flipped the switch. Nothing happened. He flipped it off again and then back on, but it was working just as it was designed.

"I sure am glad you were here this morning," he said, looking at me. It's okay if we just keep this between ourselves. No need in worrying the teachers and kids. Just one of those strange things that sometimes happen that defy explanation. You know," He said, looking at me, and I think, not believing a word he was saying but not knowing what else to say.

The truth is, I didn't know what this was all about. I like to think of myself as a practical man. I believe in God; it seems like you'd have to be crazy not to. I know there are unexplainable things that happen all over the world, or so I hear. But those things don't concern me because they are not a part of my world. But this bothered me all day. Just thinking about it made my hair raise up again as it had in Mrs. Montes' classroom. Weird. Somehow the power in that room, whatever it was, had apparently been sufficient to trip the breaker to that room. It certainly wasn't the non-existent radio. That transistor (Where did she get that old thing?) wasn't even the kind that could be hooked up to an outlet. It was battery-powered. And if the radio was as loud as Mr. McCrank said, then it couldn't have come from that little hand-held transistor. Too weird. Too weird. I didn't know it then, but a cry for help had been sent out from whatever to me. How I got in the middle of this, I didn't know, but the problem was not Mr. McCrank's to fix but mine. There was a ghost in this school house, and it was my job to clean it out. It wasn't till later that I realized that I would need a team of people to help me get it done.

Chapter 4

I saw Mr. McCrank later that day; his thin, graying hair on the top of his head was standing up like it was full of electricity. He was from the generation of Brylcreem, but I guess he had long since discontinued care. He was near retirement, and so, if you didn't like the way his hair looked, that was your problem. Anyway, he said he had gone back to Mrs. Montes's room earlier that morning. She had third-period planning and was grading papers when he walked in. She was working away, he said, totally unaware of the spooky things that were taking place in her classroom. He asked Mrs. Montes if she had left her radio on overnight.

Startled by his sudden presence, she looked up, a little perturbed at the interruption. Teachers only have this one class period to plan, or grade in this instance, and they know that what is not done then is either paid for before school or after school, at the building, or at home. In other words, on their own time. When she saw it was Mr. McCrank, the assistant principal, she dropped the frustrated look. "Umm, What radio?" She said. He walked over to the shelf and picked up the old transistor. Following her expression, he could see her confusion.

"Where did that come from?" She asked.

"Well, now, Mrs. Montes, it's in your classroom. I figured maybe it was one your father or mother had, and you had brought it to show your students. Anyway, there was a radio left in your room this morning when I got to school. I came down to shut it off, but when I opened your door, it turned off. This was the only radio I could find in your room. This is not your radio?" He asked.

"Umm, no. Mr. McCrank. When I play music, it's through my phone. I have a little speaker I use when I'm working and don't want to have my earbuds in. It has good volume, and you could possibly have heard it down the hall when you came in, only I took it home in my purse last night. My sister, Lissette, do you remember her? We both attended Patton back in the day. I think you were," she thought a minute and then said, "Weren't you a history teacher back then? I didn't have you; I had old Mrs. Akins, Lord, that woman must have taught forever, but anyway, my sister Lissette was in your class. She said that she learned a lot from you and that sometimes you were even funny. Imagine that. Anyway, she wanted to borrow it. But that little radio…I don't know where it came from. Maybe the janitor left it in here," she offered.

When Mrs. Montes, busy as she was, got rolling, it was hard to get her back on track. She was funny like that but also could lean toward annoying.

"No, I asked Larry about it this morning. Who knows how it got here. Anyway, I'll just take it out of here. No sense in it cluttering up your room. If someone comes in claiming it, just send them up to my office, and I will give it back to them." With that, he tucked the little transistor under his arm and was out the door.

"Well," I scratched my chin and said, "I wonder what Mrs. Montes was thinking about all this? Did she look spooked?"

"No, I don't think so. She seemed so busy; I'd say Mrs. Montes' didn't give it much thought. She had a class to get ready for. She did almost talk my ear off. She got started telling me about her sister, Lissette, who was in my history class a hundred years ago. I might be able to go back in one of the old yearbooks and find her, but I don't really remember her. You know, there are so many kids coming down these halls year after year. I try to learn their names. You know, Larry, you are very good at it. A person's name is music to their ears, somebody said, or something like that," he said.

As he talked with me, he pulled the old transistor out again. Where in the world did this thing come from? We were both wondering. "Hey Larry, come on down to my office, right quick. Let's see what we can find out about this thing, he said.

Alright, Mr. McCrank. I'd love to know something more about it. I have to get the shredded paper out of the mail room anyway; I said as we hustled down the hall. Inside his office, I looked about while he pulled it up on his computer screen. University of

Nebraska banners were on the wall, and a framed picture of a packed-out Memorial Stadium. "The Sea of Red" was prominent, and I could almost hear the roar of the crowd as the Big Red Machine raced out onto the field. That school used to be such a powerhouse when I was a boy. They ran up the score and were so good that there just wasn't anything anyone, except maybe Oklahoma, sometimes, could do about it. Those glory days had faded now. How in the world do we get so into sports, and especially football? It's kind of like our religion or something.

Mr. McCrank called me back to our mission at hand. "See here, Larry. This old transistor is a General Electric P-975D AM/FM Radio. Made in 1964 in Bridgeport, Connecticut. The cost was around twenty dollars. Back then, that was not cheap. Somebody likely had to save up to get this thing."

"I have one sort of like that from back in the seventies," I offered. "It's a Sanyo, though. A little handheld job. My uncle died, and he left it to me. I always liked playing with it when we went to his house. I wore that thing out. I've kept it all these years; you know, since my uncle gave it to me. His name was Rosario. People just called him 'Randy.' You know, white people, they can't seem to get these more difficult Mexican names."

"Yeah, I know white people. Except for the migrant workers, that's all that lived in Nebraska when I was growing up. I guess I would have called him Randy too. Anyway, I had one of these transistors as a kid too, but I think mine was a GE also. I think so, anyway. It's been over fifty years, Larry. Where in the world did this thing come from?" He finally asked out loud, ignoring my family history lesson.

"I don't know, boss. Maybe somehow someone is pulling a prank on us," I said, shrugging my shoulders.

He laughed when I did that. "I used to do that a lot when I was a little boy. My old granny said, "Son, you look like some crazy bird when you go around shrugging your shoulders all the time. Stop doing that." It took me a while, but I finally broke myself off it, but now, sometimes, when I see someone do that, I go back and remember Granny. Hmmm. Back to the point, if that's what it is, if someone has pulled a prank on us, Larry, they sure pulled off a good one. I know they have me more than a little shook up by this. I mean, I'm not afraid the devil is going to get me or anything, but there is something otherworldly, you know, something like spiritual worldly, it seems to me, about this whole thing," he said. He rubbed his hand over the top of his almost bald head as he said this. It reminded me of Jerry Tarkanian, the old basketball coach of UNLV when he did that. Some mental pictures seem to never go away.

I shifted around a little, and then I said, "I don't know, Mr. McCrank. All I know is I have to get back to doing something that I do understand, like cleaning urinals and sweeping tile floors. I can empty a trash can or a pencil sharpener, pick up trash on our school yard, you name it, here on our school campus, but I don't know anything about what I think you're talking about."

I could tell that he had something on his mind, and he finally burst out with it. "Larry, do you think this is some kind of spiritual thing, like a ghost trapped here or haunting or something like that?" He said.

"No, sir. I don't know anything about that. I'm just going to mind my business and get this building clean. That crazy sensation we felt in Mrs. Montes' room, I'll let you and the Ghost Busters figure that one out. If I have anything to do with it, I am just going to act like it never happened. I'm heading on into the copy room to get those bags of shredded paper to take out to recycle and then onto the more glorious parts of my job like cleaning up spills and scrubbing out urinals. Those boys down in the sixth-grade hall, we probably need to put a target on that thing. The floor seems to be wetter than the urinal, sometimes. I guess I better go see to that too, now that I think about it. I will definitely need a mop and bucket and lots of Clorox. Catch you later, Mr. McCrank," I said and headed out of there. This crazy stuff about spirits and ghosts was way out of my lane.

He chuckled. "Okay, then, Larry. You take care. Let me know if you hear of anything else going on."

"Yes, sir. I'll do that." And with that, I headed on to my duties. Little did I know what that might entail.

Chapter 5

It took a while, but I sort of forgot about all that mess. If you are in charge of keeping a whole school clean, you don't have time to be daydreaming. I mean, with over forty classrooms, the front offices, the library, and the gym, not to mention having to keep the grounds and sidewalks clean. O yeah, and the cafeteria. It's ridiculous, really. But I keep my nose to the ground and keep at it. Day after day, week after crazy week, I get it done. And I am proud of my work. I don't want folks coming in, especially the janitors from other schools, coming in and making harsh judgments on my work. You see, the city uses these school buildings for elections, boy scouts, tournaments, training for the kitchen staff, and any number of other things. People think it's just the school day I have to take care of. Wouldn't that be nice? Sometimes I work seven days a week, and, at just over ten dollars an hour, I really can't afford to complain about working so much.

Since I brought that up, let me talk to you for a minute about that. I believe that a clean and orderly school helps with work ethic. I believe it puts people in mind to want to work, or at least, it takes away the distractions of trash on the floor or sometimes the smells that go with middle school boys, especially. I do my best to keep the place looking like a place of learning. When the teachers lift their heads and remember their duty of moving these kids forward, getting them ready for high school, which means they should have as their sole purpose the goal of preparing these kids for advanced learning of some sort or other at a technical school or college. All of us together are getting these kids ready for life. For making our communities and world a place worth living and thriving in. My pay is much less than the teachers and administrators. It really should be much higher, I believe. Janitorial staff, cafeteria staff, educational assistants, bus drivers, and even librarians are not paid nearly as well as they should be. Especially if they are all working together to make these schools the training grounds they should be. Well, I've said my piece. I will retire soon, so my pay doesn't really matter too much at this point. I know for a fact that money is not a great motivator. It helps, of course, not to have to worry about making enough money to pay the bills, but the purpose is what drives people. I know my purpose here, and until the day I retire, I will achieve it to the best of my ability.

Like I was saying, I had put the spooky things out of my mind, sort of. It was the fall of the year. Halloween will be here in a few days. The kids would be getting a bit crazy thinking about it. When I was a boy, we stopped going Trick or Treat by the time we got to junior high, but it seemed like kids these days were going Trick or Treat on into high school. While I wasn't big on the foolishness of it all, the fall, and October, especially in New Mexico, are so pleasantly wonderful I could sure ask for half a year of the weather. Not too hot, not too cold, and the mosquitoes have stopped bothering by that time. Of course, nothing is ever perfect, but the weather in New Mexico in October is close enough for me. Anyway, I had just about put all this ghost business, or whatever it was, out of my mind, but then, just the other day, I overheard Mr. Rigsby and Mr. Jackson talking. They were standing outside Mr. Jackson's classroom. Mr. Rigsby serves as a special education aid to several of the teachers. He's a funny guy and very smart. He's about, say, five foot eight inches tall and has wavy hair. I guess he's about forty-five years old. He says he wants to be a nurse and is working on a nursing degree, at night, at NMU. New Mexico University has a pretty good nursing program, so he should be set up pretty well when he graduates. So many people come to work every day and do what they do, and often, unless we take time to get to know them, we don't see what their lives are really like. He and Mr. Jackson have been good friends for some time now, and it's not uncommon to see them down in the breakroom or even in Mr. Jackson's room having lunch together.

Mr. Jackson's class had been sent to lunch, and the guys were just talking. Their conversation was somewhat animated. Mr. Rigby was saying something, and you could tell by the look in his eyes that Mr. Jackson wasn't quite ready to swallow it. He sort of had that little look on his face. You know the one that says, 'O yeah, hmm. Is that so. Well, I never." Kind of mocking. Since they only have thirty minutes for lunch, I often see teachers grading papers or straightening desks, or some other tasks during their lunch while grabbing a bite of a sandwich or snack as they go. So I thought it interesting that Mr. Jackson was giving Mr. Rigsby time to talk about something he said happened in his room.

Mr. Rigsby was saying, "I had just come in the room, and I could hear your T.V. was on. When I stepped in, the screen was all snowy, but then, I know this sounds crazy, but for just a second, I thought I saw a girl in a sweatshirt hoody and, I don't know, maybe a pair of jeans. Her hair was a mess. She was looking right at me, it seemed, and then the screen flashed off."

"O man," Mr. Jackson said. When did that happen?"

"Just a few minutes ago, before your last class came in. You were standing out in the hall, getting ready for your third-period students, and I had stepped in to put my stuff down. You didn't hear the T.V. on"? Mr. Rigsby asked.

"No, no, I didn't. Mr. Rigsby that is creepy," he said. The mocking look he had earlier was now gone and gave way to a look of concern.

"Yeah, and it's not like the T.V. was just on, and a girl was on the screen. I mean, it looked like she was looking straight at me," Mr. Rigsby said, his eyes begging to be believed.

"I'm sure glad you didn't tell me that before class. I'm not sure I could have held it together enough to teach the lesson,' Mr.

Jackson replied. That is the craziest thing I've ever heard. What did the girl look like? I know you said she had a sweatshirt hoody on and jeans, and her hair was all a mess. How old was she? Was she Anglo or Spanish?"

Just then, they noticed that I had stopped dead in my track. It was like I couldn't move.

"Hey, have you ever heard of anything like that going on at this school, Mr. Rodriguez? I mean, you've been working here a while. What do you think of that story?" Mr. Jackson asked me. Mr. Jackson was older, about my age, mid to late fifties. He was taller than Mr. Rigsby, I guess about five foot eleven inches, or even six feet. He always wore glasses and sort of reminded me of a teacher from a cartoon I had seen kids watching sometime or other. Always wore button-up collared shirts and dress pants. He was a kindly man, and I always felt comfortable around him.

There was no use pretending I hadn't been listening. "Hey, fellows, Sorry for listening in. I just, well, I haven't heard anything just like that. No, nothing just like that. Probably just a glitch in the electrical system or something. You boys have a nice lunch. I, I have to uh, get over to Mr. McCrank's office. He has a spill or something. I'll see you guys later." Then I was off down the hall a bit quicker than I meant to go. I left them staring after me. What was going on? Shoot! I don't know what to think about all these happenings. It had been a few weeks since that episode in Mrs.

Montes' classroom, and I was just about ready to just chalk it up to just another weird thing that happened sometimes but now… Maybe Mr. McCrank will be able to help me figure it out. I sure need someone to talk to about it.

Chapter 6

"Mr. McCrank is doing lunch duty right now," Ms. Riana, the office receptionist, told me. "He should be back in his office around one, I guess," she said. Ms. Riana was always nice and informed, which made her the perfect person for the front desk. She had boatloads of people coming through there every day, and somehow or another, she seemed to keep smiling. You have to give kudos to people like that.

There was too much to do to wait for Mr. McCrank right now. Ms. Philpot had asked me earlier to bring in an extra desk for her classroom. Sixth-grade students sometimes had a hard time adapting to middle school routines, and she had this one boy who had moved in from out of state…Well, needless to say, it was going to take a bit of training for this one. And she also had a couple of desks that weren't balancing right. They kept rocking back and forth. Sixth graders have enough trouble concentrating, but when their desks rock, well, that's a whole new game. And then there was the hourly bathroom sweep that I do, making sure someone hadn't rolled out all the toilet paper or thrown up. Sometimes my job is pretty gross, I won't go into any details just now, but I have done the job long enough that it really doesn't bother me much anymore. The key to this kind of work, like any, I suppose, is to keep your head down and your nose to the grindstone. In other words, keep at it. Quit telling yourself that it will take forever and that the work in front of you is impossible, and just do it. I am amazed at how much can be done when people just stay with something and don't wear themselves out complaining about it. Tenacity. I guess maybe that word could be the key to success in anything in life. Maybe all of life itself.

I know I ramble some. Sorry about that. Anyway, I headed out of the office and suddenly remembered I hadn't eaten. In fact, besides a cup of coffee this morning before I left the house, I hadn't eaten since last night when I came in from work. My stomach growled at me, reprimanding me for my forgetfulness. I headed over to the janitor's closet, where I kept my lunch box. It was one of those old-school ones that clipped shut in the front, sort of like a toolbox. Inside, in the lid, was a place for a thermos. I would often fill it with coffee from the teacher's lounge at lunch. By then, most of the teachers had gotten their daily allowance of coffee. Today I had peanut butter and jelly, my old standby, and a few of those vanilla cookies I have always liked since I was a kid. Crazy how something that most people might think of as a sort of a last resort kind of food option could become important to others by some memory association from the past. I took these cookies to school with me when I went to school in Palomas all those years ago. Being brought up with less than some had been more than enough for me. In retrospect, I didn't ever remember feeling like I didn't have enough or was being left out of the good things in life. My Abuela, especially, always helped us to see that we were blessed beyond measure. "We serve a God with an open hand. We have to make sure that our hands aren't full of a bunch of stuff that doesn't matter, so we can receive the true riches offered to our hands from His." She was the godliest of women.

Sitting down in the teacher's lounge, I took my sandwich out of the bag and placed it on a napkin. I took my coffee thermos and filled it with what remained of the morning coffee. It grows stronger as the day goes by, and I always need a good shot by this time of day. I kept a coffee mug up in the cabinet and used it from time to time, especially if I forgot my lunch or accidentally left the thermos out. When I used it, I washed it up nice and placed it back in the lounge cabinet in a special place back in the corner. No one ever touched it. It was always right where I left it. Funny, but such a small thing as this gave me a feeling of respect and belonging somehow. Little things...In the mornings, Mr. McCrank or I always got the coffee going for teachers to have available when they came in. It was a twenty-cup pot, so most days, there was still some left over when I finally got down to the lounge for my lunch. Today was no different. I sat down and ate my lunch, thanking God for the few minutes of solitude before getting back at it. I almost always take my lunch after all the kids and teachers have had theirs. That gives me the benefit of this quiet time. Nice. I learned the hard way that taking my lunch earlier more than half the time meant getting interrupted to have to go clean up some spill in the cafeteria or something or other. I had had enough of that. Today, halfway into my sandwich and cup of coffee, however, Mrs. Douglass came in to heat up a bowl of soup she had brought from home. She was the librarian who almost never left her librarian domain, even taking most of her lunches there, continuing to be available to her students and teachers that might come in during her lunch break. She had just been hired the year before, replacing a lady who had been there several years before she went and got herself married and hustled off by her new husband someplace north and west of New Mexico. I think it might have been Washington State, but I can't remember for sure. Anyway, Mrs. Douglass had moved in here determined to fill big shoes and, despite her valiant efforts and upbeat spirit, was having a hard time gaining acceptance from the old heads, especially the women teachers. What was she supposed to do? She was not the cause of the other librarian leaving. Anyway, who can understand group dynamics?

"O, Hello. How are you, Mrs. Douglass?" I said, wiping my mouth with my napkin and pushing back a little from the table.

"Doing fine, Mr. Rodriguez. You finally get a break?" She asked.

"Well, that's sort of the pot calling the kettle black, but Yes, Ma'am. It's been a busy morning, but it's all good. It will be another day over before you know it. O, and Mrs. Douglass, you can just call me Larry. That's what everyone else calls me. Mr. Rodriguez is my dad."

"Okay, Larry. I don't want to get you confused with your dad."

"Don't get me wrong. My dad was a fine man, and if I measure up to him, I will do very well. I guess the truth is I don't deserve to be called by the same name. So, thank you, Mrs. Douglass. I appreciate it."

She looked at me like he had maybe given her a plateful when she had only asked for one side. "Hey, Larry, are you really busy today?" She asked.

"No, ma'am. Not any more than any other day. What can I do for you?" I felt foolish for going on about my dad and our name and everything. I've been thinking about family a lot lately, especially with Dia de los Muertos coming up. It sort of had me off balance, I guess.

"Well, I must have a couple of loose shelves in the library. Every morning when I come in, there are books falling off in the floor. I pick them up and put them back in their proper place, God bless the Dewey Decimal System, but then they are back on the floor the next morning. I checked it myself, but I couldn't tell that any of the shelves were loose, but I was hoping maybe you could see if you could figure it out." She asked.

I must have got this strange look on my face because Mrs. Douglass said, "Don't worry about it, Larry. I didn't mean to overwhelm you with just one more thing to do."

"No, no, it's okay, Mrs. Douglass. I was just thinking of something all of a sudden. I will be in there just as soon as I put my lunch box up, so I don't forget."

"I appreciate it, Larry. See you soon." With that, she was out the door, back to the grind, I guess.

I sat there just amazed at the compilation of events that were there in front of me all of a sudden. How long had this been going on? Mrs. Douglass said it was happening day after day in the library. Had I been so busy that I couldn't see the evidence before me? Something was going on here, and it was beginning to creep me out. With that thought, I felt a cold chill up my back. "I must be going nuts," I told myself. I put my cup in the sink. I'd wash it later. I grabbed my lunch box and started to hustle it down to my closet, but then thought better of it and left it on the counter by the coffee pot. I had to get to the library and get to the bottom of this. The library was just down the hall a bit from the teacher's lounge, so I went straight there.

Mrs. Douglass looked up when I came through the library door. She usually had classes in there, checking out books or reading quietly. Today was no different. It was Mr. Allen's seventh-grade language arts class. He made his kids toe the line.

All of them were working quietly, either reading or writing down information from the books they were working with. From the looks of it, they were doing research on various types of horses, mules, and donkeys.

I walked over to Mrs. Douglass's desk. She had this big picture of a sunflower posted beside her desk. I suppose one of the students had drawn it for her. Whispering, I said, "Hey, this is not bad. One of your students make this for you?"

"O, my sunflower? I just love that. Yeah, it was a little Rodriguez boy in sixth grade that drew that for me. His name is Julio. See? He even signed it for me. I had told the students that I was from Kansas when I introduced myself this year, and the next day, he brought this drawing of a sunflower to me. I just couldn't believe the detail, especially since you don't see many of them around here," she said, looking adoringly at the drawing. With praise from staff coming in such short doses, praise received must be relished. There was a time when I could feel that myself.

"Hmm, a Rodriguez boy. With a name like that, he has to be okay, right?" I said with a wink.

"I guess so. You know those Rodriguez'. Always so kind and thoughtful," she said, smiling back.

"Well, now, all of a sudden, it is getting pretty deep in here. I might need to go get my muck boots," I said. We both laughed. "Anyway, show me these shelves. You've got me curious."

Mrs. Douglass led me over to the poetry section. Right about here and here," she motioned with her hands. Almost every morning. The crazy thing is, no matter how many books are down, Shakespeare's Hamlet and Edgar Allen Poe's The Complete Tales and Poems are always on the ground. Isn't that crazy?"

"I'd say. Let's just check here. I want to set these books off and see if maybe one of the shelf pegs has worked loose or something," I said.

"Okay. Here, let me set them out, Larry. You know that Dewey Decimal System. I'll just set them out in groups." She got down on her knees on the carpeted floor, taking her time, being sure to keep the books in proper order. "There. Now you can check it. I should have done that," she said.

I wiggled them back and forth. I got down and looked underneath. I even took the shelf board out and put it back in again.

"Hmm. It doesn't seem to be loose. Let me check this other one. Here, hand me those books, and I'll put them back on the shelf," I said.

"No, I'll take care of this, Larry. You just check on that other one there. Thanks," she replied.

I checked the second set of shelves, doing the same as I had on the other one, making sure everything was secure.

"It looks like this one is okay, too." Having seen her diligence to be precise, I put the books down in the precise order they were on the shelf. She moved over and saw how neatly I had placed them there.

"Thanks for keeping the books in order so nicely. I got busy over at the other shelf and had forgotten. But not to worry. You did this just right. Thanks."

"You bet. We didn't have many books at home growing up, so when we went to the library, it was sort of like going into a church, you know. I always felt good there," I said.

"If only the kids of an entitled age felt the same way. Thanks for saying that, Mr. Rodriguez. I know you are not your dad, but that comment qualifies you for more respect than the name Larry seems to offer. "

I had started to correct her, but after her little speech, I just smiled and thanked her.

"I'm sorry I didn't find anything, Mrs. Douglass. I'll be sure to check back here tomorrow morning and see if they are down again. I bet one of the kids is sneaking in here somehow and doing it. I don't really see how but there has to be an explanation for it," I said with a shrug off my shoulders, remembering what Mr. McCrank said earlier and stopped.

"Thanks, Larry. I appreciate you taking a look. See you later. And sorry for interrupting your lunch," she said.

"Okay, Mrs. Douglass. Any time." With that, I walked quietly past Mr. Allen's class and out the door. His kids were now diligently getting notes from their books about horses. It was cool seeing them research things that seem to matter more, at least to me. I had always loved nature and animals, all gifts from the hand of God. Man, with all his initiative, had never matched the incredible designs of his Maker. God is good. The janitor from back in the day, the mystery of Mrs. Montes' room, Mr. Rigsby and Mr. Jackson's room story, and now this with Mrs. Douglass in the library. I still didn't make the connections that would come later, but I knew there were strange things happening that needed an answer.

Chapter 7

I stepped outside to get some fresh air before I got started over in the cafeteria cleaning up after the kids. I guessed I'd have to catch up with Mr. McCrank after school now, with his busy schedule and mine, but, boy, did I have a lot I wanted to talk to him about.

It was the end of October. I have been to many places over my lifetime. I have been blessed to see God's handiwork in many states and a few countries. That being said, anytime I have been anywhere in October, I have stood in awe. It's like this is the crescendo of beauty all over the world. It is certainly no different here. The air is fresh, and the leaves of the trees are magnificent. The breeze was just slight enough to take the cool of the day and make me want to brush my arms with my hands. Brrrr. Not freezing or anything, just fresh. You know. O, how I love October! I was born for this. Sometimes I think wouldn't it be great if it stayed like this all the time? Just to be able to hike every hill and see every valley during this time when the air smells of the earth as she lays her summer dress aside and lets us see things unseen and forgotten for most of the year. Yes, sir, I love it, but the truth is, without the bitter cold of winter and the scorching heat of summer, spring and fall wouldn't come across so spectacular. O, to have eyes to see the beauty in all of it!

Eyes are what I need now. How to see what was going on and make some sense of it. I mean, I know it's October. Halloween and all that. But I don't believe in all that, or at least, I didn't.

The day passed in a blur. It seemed to me that it was just over, but somehow, I had cleaned up in the cafeteria, done my bathroom checks, and got the wiggly desks set right. These old desks have held up remarkably, but after a while, things are going to be broken or misaligned. That's just the way it is. That's kind of the way I was feeling right now. Maybe I have been working, working, working too long and just need a break. Surely all these events were just my tired mind chewing on things that needed to just be let go. Coincidence. That's all. I decided right then and there that I wasn't even going to tell Mr. McCrank about all these other happenings in the school unless he brought it up. He might have just been pulling my leg about what happened in Mrs. Montes' room. Mr. Rigby is just blowing to pass the time with Mr. Jackson, and Mrs. Douglass' books being off the shelf is just the act of some mischievous middle schooler. However, I must say that if Mr. McCrank was messing with me, he sure is a good actor. But that's what it is. Mr. McCrank, you old devil. You played a good one on me, maybe even got Mr. Rigsby and Mr. Jackson in on it. Still, I can't believe that Mrs. Douglass was messing with me. She...no, she was legit. But then again. No. The whole mess in the library is just some kid, as I thought. Rodriguez, man, you are going to have to just chill. Why don't you give your wife a call? You know, just unwind and see what she's into. You know, you're right. Yeah, that is just what I will do. I'll give my wife a call and tell her not to worry about making supper. I'll stop by Ranchway, this kind of hole-in-the-wall Mexican place over on Valley, and grab us some chicken enchiladas with onions and egg on top. Of course, they always have their beans and rice on the side. It will be delicious. I'll even get us a couple of sopapillas with honey. In my opinion, it is one of the best restaurants in town, and their prices don't put a hole in your pocketbook either. The truth is, my wife could even put them out of business with her cooking, but I want to give her a break today. Shoot, I might even get some flowers and take them home to her. I can't remember when I did that last. I just work too much, and it seems like that is all I ever think about. My wife deserves someone better than me. Maybe tonight I can make it up to her.

It was thinking like this that just made the day disappear. I was halfway through the classrooms in the language arts and history wing when I sort of woke up out of my dream. Everyone was gone. Many of the teachers will work till past suppertime, some nights. There have been times when I have had to run them out. "Sorry, Ms. Reynolds, I have to lock up now." "Umm, Mr. Wilson, anything I can help you with? It's time for me to lock up." They always seem to be confused that I am even there. Like my day today, they get lost in their work and wonder where the time went. Of course, there are some lazy teachers, just there to draw a paycheck, there's always going to be some of those in every kind of work, but some of these teachers are so dedicated to their work and this school and these children, that money has little to do with it. Gotta love that kind of teacher.

I went down to the teacher's lounge and went into the little conference calling room. Most teachers use their cell phones anymore to make calls home. Somehow, they block their numbers so they don't get those weird calls back late at night. The room was vacant, as I expected, so I popped in there to make my call.

"Hey, honey. Is everything okay?" My wife asked when I called.

"Yeah, sure. I was just wondering if you'd like to take the night off from cooking supper and let me bring us something home. What do you think?" I asked.

"Sounds good to me. I already had supper rolling, but I can put it away for tomorrow. What's the occasion? I don't think it's our anniversary." She said back to me.

"No, no, nothing like that. Can't a guy just bring his favorite woman a bite to eat sometimes just to show her he appreciates her?" I said. Smiling to myself for finally thinking of my wife for a change.

"As I said, sounds good to me." She returned.

"I was just working away up here, and I got to thinking about how blessed I am to have such a wonderful wife. And then I felt ashamed because I hardly ever show you how much I appreciate you. It's time I did differently." I kind of felt all mushy saying all that, but it was most definitely true. When you've got a good woman, you better let her know. You don't want her getting her compliments from some other man. You be the man; you know what I mean?

"You know, you better be careful, Mr. Rodriguez, or you might end up spoiling your woman," she teased.

"It's a chance I'm willing to take, ma'am," I said and hung up the phone.

When I got off the phone, I headed out to the truck. The night air was cool, and I wished I had grabbed a jacket. Tomorrow I would definitely bring at least a windbreaker. The stars were shining brightly, and I could already see the planet Mars and then the Archer laying on his back. I saw the Seven Sisters, faintly as always. The night sky is glory and a gift from God that I seldom lift my eyes to see. As I went to open the door, there was a cool breeze that came up on me, more than just the night air. It chilled me to the bone so much that I wrapped my arms around myself, brushing my hands quickly up and down my arms to get my blood flowing, and then quickly got the door open and jumped inside. Man, I wanted to get this thing fired up and the heater rolling. I hadn't had the heater on so far this year. In New Mexico, the temperatures don't drop so drastically, except when these crazy northern storms sweep in; they sometimes will drop down way out of Canada and freeze us up as well. I think it was 2009 when that big freeze dropped down on us in February and killed a lot of the palm trees and burst people's water lines everywhere. I mean, the temperatures are so mild, usually in the southern part of the state, that folks don't even wrap their pipes and put those covers on the outside spickets as they do up north. So, even though it was very deep into the month of October, I hadn't needed my truck's heater, but I was sure going to fire it up tonight. Brrrr!

The dusty smell of a heater that hadn't been used for a season rose up in my truck. This old 93 F150 4x4 had been mine for years. It only had one hundred thousand miles on it when I got it. I know, you say, "Only a hundred thousand miles!" but remember, I'm a school janitor, knocking around twenty-five thousand a year, and that's with overtime and picking up jobs when some other school needs help. You do what you can, know what I mean? Besides, this old truck is a classic, it gets me where I'm going, and it's a man's truck, you know. Sure, I've had to do work on it: replaced the tires right off, changed the oil and filter, air filter, fuel filter, and serpentine belt. It wasn't long before I had to replace the battery and, just last year, the starter. I have been hearing this kind of sick sound in it from time to time lately, so I figure my alternator will be going soon, but hey, all that's just the small stuff.

Between Auto Zone and O'Reilly's, we're all sort of on a first-name basis. Anyway, because it's got a few dings and the paint is faded on the cab and hood, I can take it off-road, load gravel or concrete, or mesquite bushes, and so what? It doesn't matter. It's a work truck, and I like it that way. And you know what? It cost me twenty-seven hundred dollars. I paid in cash. If I went over to the Ford dealership today and said give me one of those new F150 4x4s, they'd be happy to help me take out a loan for the seventy months it would take to pay off the Thirty-five thousand I'd have to borrow to get it. You won't catch this old boy doing that! The borrower is a slave to the lender, the Proverbs say. I'd say King Solomon got that right!

I had my radio tuned into KGRT, a local country station, as I drove over to Ranchway. "The Ride" came across the waves, and I listened to David Allan Coe sing about the ghost of Hank Williams, Sr. a guy named Gary Gentry wrote that song after he saw a shirtless Hank Williams, Sr. sitting on a couch down the hall in the living room. Of course, he does say that he was drinking rather heavily back in those days, so take that for what it's worth. He did write a cool country song from his experience, though. I thought it was interesting that that particular song came on during my short ride to Ranchway. It is over twenty years old, after all. And KGRT does play country music but is not known for playing the oldies. It's always saying, "Playing today's country music."

Anyway, it just kind of struck me as strange after everything else that has happened today.

Ranchway has an extra gravel lot for parking, and since I was getting there around supper time, the place was pretty well packed. Anticipating this kind of crowd, I had called from the school before I left and ordered my enchiladas to go. The tables were full of families and couples and a few business types in their suits and fancy dresses. I checked in at the register and made sure they had my order and then kind of hung around looking at the pictures they had hanging on the wall. They have some bullfighters and senoras and rodeo rider paintings. O, and they have this cool one with a Mexican cowboy wrangling a bronco—super cool. I would hang that one in my garage where I work on things if it were mine. Kind of makes me feel macho or something. It makes time pass just being able to look at these elements of Mexican culture while you wait. Just as you are coming in, they have these pictures of Pancho Villa. He is sort of a hero to some of the Kids of Mexican descent in the public schools. You say, "Pancho Villa," and they say, "Pancho Villa! Aha!" In reality, he was like a terrorist before the term was cool. He invaded Columbus, New Mexico, in 1916, I think, looking for guns. General Pershing of the U.S. Army chased him all over, even into Mexico, I believe, but he never caught him. There is a restaurant down in Palomas, Mexico, called the Tienda Rosa that has a statue of Pancho Villa and General Pershing shaking hands like they became friends later on or something. I don't know if they did or not. My people are from Palomas, so I kind of get homesick when I see these pictures of the part of Mexico where I grew up. These were my heroes. Men who were tough, who lived hard and died hard too, sometimes. And you know, when I was a boy, talk of Pancho wasn't so much like he was a hero or something. We knew he was up to no good, but it is just the idea of the little man punching back at the overwhelming odds he faces. It shows a spirit that we want to harvest and bring up in ourselves and our children. I don't know if that makes any sense or not. It's kind of complicated, like so much of life.

Anyway, as I was looking at the photos, I noticed Villa's big sombrero and his ribbons of bullets draped across his chest this way and that. He was smiling through his bushy mustache as he stood there with several of his men. What had driven him to such extremes? Surely, he was just another little boy running the dusty streets of Northern Mexico. Surely his momma made tortillas every morning, and he ate nopalitos almost every night. Everybody else is keeping their heads down, as they are expected to do, but he just does his own thing. One hundred years later, all the rest have turned to dust, but his legacy lives on. When it comes to living, which way is better? Sometimes I guess I don't really know. Right now, it's like I'm this detective or something, and I have this great lead for breaking the case, but I am not sure if I should pursue it or not. After all, I am not a detective. I am a school janitor. Like Villa, I'm supposed to keep my head down. I am supposed to clean toilets and sweep up gyms, not get to the bottom of whether spirits roam the hallways of Patton Middle School. I really do just need to chill out. The cashier broke me out of my rabbit chasing. That's what I call it when my mind just takes one trial after another, the results of which could lead me anywhere.

"Number 17," He called. "Chicken enchiladas with egg and onions."

"Right here," I answered back. "Yes, sir. Thank you."

You pay first at Ranchway. You order and pick up from the same guy. It's a kind of a hole in the wall like I said, but it sure is good. I took my order, which comes in those white Styrofoam boxes all tucked into a plastic bag with the double handles on it, and nodded to those who looked up at me as I made my way out to the parking lot.

I headed out to the truck. Remember, I had parked out in the extended gravel lot because there was such a big crowd when I got there. The parking lot had thinned a little while I waited. It was nearing seven, and the rush for a good Mexican meal on a weeknight had calmed. The cool of a late October evening was in the air and all over me. I got in the truck and cranked it up. My radio blared at me, full blast. I quickly reached over and cut the volume way down. What the hey? I mean, I was just listening to KGRT and country music. I might have had the radio turned up a little to rise up over the sound of an old truck engine and a little exhaust leak I have just behind the cab, but this was ridiculous. Come on, man. Then I saw the dial was set to 93.1, KISS-FM. How did I get to that station? The adult contemporary mix is a far cry from Today's Country. I started to tune back into KGRT when on a whim, I turned the volume up to hear what was playing. "Thriller" by Michael Jackson was playing. You talk about creepy. I mean, is it just a coincidence that two ghost songs on two different stations, one of which I hadn't even intentionally tuned into, were coming across the waves after all the business I have been dealing with today? And both of these songs are way over twenty years old. I really have to get home. I know I will tell my wife. Maybe not, no, definitely not the whole day's business; it would make her think I'd lost it, but even though it would probably be best if I just kept it to myself, I know I will tell my Rosa. It has always been that way. She listens. Often without comment.

We lived just outside of town in the little village of Dona Ana. There used to be more of a town presence there, but now it was just the cotton gin, one of four left in the county. And there is the guy that replaces windshields. He has a little business out of his house. I suppose there may be another place or two like that, but if there is, I don't know about it. Right before I passed the last signal light on the way out of town, I remembered the flowers. "Shoot! I meant to get flowers for my wife. Dog gone it! I whipped the truck around and drove back down to Save Mart on Valley. Even though it is a locally owned grocery store, it should have a few bouquets of flowers to choose from. I think they are still open. Surely. When I pulled into the parking lot, I could see there were still a few cars in the parking lot. Hopefully not just employees cleaning up or restocking the shelves.

I jumped out of the truck and hustled up to the door. The sign read seven am to eight pm, Sunday through Saturday. While I am for people taking a break and getting away from their work, I sure do love consistency. You can rely on it, you know. I like that. Good old Save Mart.

The black mat under me initiated the opening of the door. Thank goodness. I wasn't too late. As soon as I stepped in, I saw the flowers up by the register. There was just one bunch remaining. A dozen white roses. I had in my mind a dozen red roses, but these would do. Better something than nothing, I figure. Of course, my wife wouldn't be expecting flowers, but that will make it all the better. I lifted the flowers up out of their holder, water dripping from the stems, and slipped them in this little clear plastic bag hanging there for that purpose. No need to get the passenger seat wet. As I checked out with the flowers, the girl at the register rang them up and gave me my total.

"Where did you find these?" She asked.

"They were just right here. They were the only ones you had left. I had really hoped for red ones, but these will do," I said, smiling.

"That's funny," she said. I don't remember seeing them up here. I thought we sold out of flowers before I took my lunch break. Hmm, I'd say it's because I have been too busy, but the truth is it's been nothing but crickets in here this evening. I don't know where everyone is. If it was Friday night, I would blame it on the football games, but the week's just getting started well. Anyway, weird. I have swept up around here several times tonight; that's how slow it is. You know how the boss always says, "At least look busy," but I haven't seen those flowers till just now. I guess I wasn't looking for them. You know what they say. Keep your head down, and nobody gets hurt," she said.

"Is that what they say? Things sure are changing. Hey, well, hmmm." I noticed her name tag read 'Jenny,' so I said, "Hey, Jenny, I bet you're a student up here at Mayfield, right? That would explain it. Not that Mayfield students are dumb or anything like that; I just mean, you must have homework you're mulling over or have a boyfriend you're thinking about. Yeah, I bet that's it," I said, a bit nervous now. I really shouldn't have said that last part. If she doesn't have a boyfriend, it might make her sad, especially on a slow night, about how she doesn't have a boyfriend waiting for her when she gets off. O, the drama of being a teenager. Thank you, Lord, that you helped me make it past all that! I thought to myself.

"No, not really. I mean, I am a student, but I don't have any homework I am concerned about, and I don't even have a ghost of a boyfriend," she said back. "I mean, it's not like I haven't had boyfriends. O yeah, I've had plenty of boyfriends. The fact is I'm about tired of the whole drama of what is he thinking and does he like my hair, and "Momma, I promise we're not doing anything,' all that jazz." Just then, she looked up from her monologue. She must have noticed my startled look because she said, "Are you alright, mister? Maybe you shouldn't be driving."

"What? No, I'm fine; it was just something you said that made me remember something, that's all. I'm fine, really. Have a good rest of your night, Jenny," I said. I grabbed my flowers and started toward the door.

"Are you sure, mister? My dad will be here to pick me up in half an hour or so. We could drive you home if, if…." She stumbled, trying to find the right words.

"I'm fine. Really, thanks," I said and made a dash for the door. I went out into the now cold October night. This is getting a little bit too strange. I have got to get home. Good night; I have never had so many threads in a singular theme in my life. I jumped in the truck and headed back out on Valley Drive, going north toward Dona Ana. Thankfully the radio was right where I left it. "Highwayman" came on. Jennings, Nelson, Cash, Kristofferson. I reached over and turned it off. "Lord," I said. "Somehow or another, I have to get home. I have never believed in ghosts, but creepy things are happening today. I would sure appreciate it if you would help me get my mindset right. My poor wife will be scared to death if I go home telling her all this madness. Shoot, I'm getting pretty scared myself. Don't, don't' let me show that. Lord, I'll let you go now, but please send me some protection from whatever is going on. Thanks. Thanks in advance, Jesus. Amen." The winds were pushing my truck a bit sideways when I turned toward home. There surely must be a storm blowing in, I thought to myself.

The next thing I knew, I was pulling into my gravel driveway. I could see the lights on in the house. You don't know how relieved I was just to be at home. I popped the door open and hopped out. The winds were picking up and blew my driver's door back on my leg. Ouch! What else is going to happen tonight? Pushing it back, I grabbed our supper and the flowers. The night Chilling air was something else now. It was stirring and swirling around and cold! We get dust devils in New Mexico. They blow dirt and trash all around. They can reach way up in the sky like a funnel cloud too, but I've only ever seen them during the daytime. I guess it makes sense that they come at night also. This at least felt like one coming up on me. The branches of the mulberry trees were dancing all around me. I turned my back to the wind and sheltered the food and flowers. The last thing we needed was sand all in our food and stems where the flowers had been.

My wife met me at the door. She had turned the outside light on for me, thankfully. Her hair was blowing in the wind, and she shouted over it to tell me, "Hurry and get in here!" When I went inside, I put the food on the kitchen table and presented her with the white roses.

"For you, my dear," I said. Her face turned from smiling and welcoming to ashen. She brushed her hair out of her face, and I saw her eyes go from the flowers to my face and then back again. My smile in presenting the flowers melted away.

"Where did you get those?" She said, trembling. I didn't know what the deal was, but this was not the response that I had hoped for.

"Umm, I got them at Save Mart. I wanted to surprise you. I told you I would bring in our supper, but I wanted more than that, so I stopped by and picked up these flowers. Why, Honey? What's wrong?"

Her face changed, and then she said, "O, Honey. You are so thoughtful, and the food smells delicious. Thank you. I don't know what I was thinking," she said, brushing my question aside.

"Okay then," I said. It seemed like something else strange was going on, but I had had quite a day and didn't really have the energy to pursue it. I said a quick prayer quietly to myself, "Lord, let everything go right tonight, please?"

She took the flowers from me and then took my hand, and we went over to the table to sit down. We opened those little Styrofoam boxes they put the take-out food in and broke out the plasticware. No dishes tonight.

"Honey, I have had the strangest day. I will have to tell you about it later, maybe after we go to bed. But right now, I'm starved, and this smells great. I just want to tell you before we eat that you are a remarkable woman and I am a very lucky man. This was all just meant to tell you that. I love you," I leaned over and kissed her. She smiled back at me and said, "Larry, you are the best husband ever. It's me that needs to tell you that more." And we just dug into our food. As I think back over it now, there was a certain look in her eyes that was somehow out of place, but I just wasn't wise enough to discern it back then. I believe in God and take my faith seriously. Maybe that was evidenced by all the praying I was doing tonight. I pray every day and ask God to bless me in my work and help me to honor him in all that I do. When people tell me of troubles in their lives or things they are thankful for, I join them in praying for help or praising God for his blessings, but I have been praying much more than usual today. I should have mustered up the energy to ask God to help me understand what was going on with my wife when I got home. I should have, but I was just too tired.

Chapter 8

When I got up this morning, I felt much better. "I decided to light it up and let it go." That's a phrase they kept trying to pass over to the teachers in those meetings they had at the beginning of the year. "Don't stress. Just let it go. We will all get through this together," They say. Well, the beginning of the year surely is a stressful time. Lots of parents bring their kids in to register them on the first day, and students not being able to read their schedules or understand where they are supposed to go from here. Lots of crazy stuff. Then there's us janitors who are having to get new desks because now this teacher just got two more kids than the original printout or the spills and, well, you get it. Craaazy.

But today, I figured, I was just going to start over. Surely all that far-out business of yesterday was just a man who was a bit too tired and stressed. I got up around five thirty, like usual, and got the coffee brewing. If I can get a good cup of coffee in me, and especially if I can just kick back a little and just really think about nothing. You know. I love it when I can just feel that cool autumn air and kind of find my place in the world. The Bible says in Acts 17:24, "The God who made the world and everything in it is the Lord of heaven and earth and does not live in temples built by human hands." I can get that. I mean, when I have time to just stop for a minute and see and feel the beauty that is all around me, I sense his presence. I don't have to go to some special place for that. He is here with me now. I really need that assurance as I get my boots and jeans on and head out the door. Too many nutty things going on at the school not to have some anchor to hold onto when the storm cranks up and rocks my world. I'm just out the door when my wife calls after me. She is in her nightgown and this warm plush lavender robe I gave her for Christmas last year. "Honey," she calls.

I look up, surprised. Usually, she sleeps in a bit on school days, so I get about the house quietly, trying not to wake her. I guess I failed at that this morning. "Good morning, Rosa. I'm sorry I woke you," I say.

"No, no. I've been awake. I wanted to thank you again for last night and apologize for not showing you more appreciation. Larry, I love you! Hurry home to me this evening. I'll have a nice supper fixed for you. I want you to know how much I appreciate you," she said. She gives me this little look sometimes; I really can't describe it. It is peculiar to her. Somehow, she purses her lips, and I know that she is my Rosa. Mine and mine alone. What a woman she is.

"I love you too, Rosa. I'll get home to you as quick as I can tonight," I said as I turned and hurried on to get my truck going. It was cool out, and that heater would get fired up again this morning. I am so glad to have a wife that appreciates me and a truck that has a heater that works. What else could a man want, really?

Well, anyway, new day. As I drive into work, the dawn falls over town and the glow of the new morning begins to show on the autumn leaves. It's pretty magnificent. I pull into the parking lot of the school and see that Mr. McCrank is already there again. It's not yet six thirty, but he likes to get at it. I like the old crank and have a great appreciation for his devotion to the school.

When I go into the building, I don't see Mr. McCrank, so I head back to the janitor's closet and put my lunch box away. Next, I head into the teacher's lounge to make sure Mr. McCrank has gotten the coffee going. I smell that Folgers as I open the door and know he's beaten me to it once again. The pot is still brewing, or I might be tempted to sit down and have another cup. Better I don't anyway. I need to go unlock a couple of the classrooms. Mrs. Montes and Mr. Phillips have both called in sick and won't be in today. I need to make sure the doors are open so their subs can come in and get everything set up.

Mr. Phillips is in the sixth-grade hall, so since that's closest to the teacher's lounge, I head there first. Everything is quiet in the sixth-grade hall. I take a look at a new bulletin board one of the teachers has put up. It's a fall display with a tree in the center that has Ms. Banister's name printed on the trunk and then the names of students on the leaves of the trees. Some of the leaves are still on the tree, and some have fallen on the ground. It reads, "Fall into learning." That's a catchy little phrase. As I walk on down the hall, I wonder how she determined which students to leave on the tree and which ones to place on the ground. Is there any symbolism there? Is it better to have been a leaf that has reached full maturity and has fallen on the ground or to be one that is still clinging to the tree? Then again, maybe I am over-analyzing a cute poster designed for sixth graders.

I look at my watch and see that it is nearing seven. Mr. Jackson is coming down the science hall, headed for his classroom. His classroom is called "the Chapel" because it used to be two sped classrooms, so it arched up in the middle where the sliding curtain used to be. It's kind of appropriate, I guess because he used to be a preacher or priest or something, I think. Anyway, he says, "Good morning, Larry! It sure is beautiful outside today!" He is always like that, you know. Brings sunshine into the room kind of person. Who couldn't like that? Unless, of course, you are in a grouchy mood and don't want anyone spoiling your fun. I have heard teachers talking about him after he greets them with his bright smile and upbeat talk. They say things like, "Just one time, I'd like to see that guy come in here in a sour mood so the rest of us could just go on about our miserable lives without his blather. He can't be happy all the time."

I return his greeting. "Hey, Mr. Jackson. You got that right. Another beautiful day in New Mexico! How good can it get?" He beams at my response. I figure if you can't beat 'em, join 'em. He has on his tennis shoes along with dress pants and a button-up collared shirt. He always dresses nice, except the tennis shoes seem to go against his clothing choice. To me, they seem to go better with jeans, which the teachers can only wear on Fridays and field trips. I asked him about it one day, and he said when he first started teaching, he wore dress shoes. Every day he went home with his legs cramping and his feet killing him. One day he had had enough and put his running shoes on to wear to school. He said he had the best day teaching since he had begun. He said, "If your feet hurt, it's mighty hard to put on a happy face." Ever since that day, he has been a happy tennis shoe wearer. His story must be true because he comes practically skipping down the hall to his room every morning. That Mr. Jackson is quite a character.

When I get to Mrs. Montes' room, I notice that the door is already open. O boy, I think, here we go again. I know I said I wasn't going to think about the events of yesterday, but this immediately gets my guard up. I push open the door, and there stands Mr. McCrank. He doesn't even hear me come in.

"Mmmm, good morning, Mr. McCrank. How's the morning going?" I ask.

Startled, he looks up. His face is white and lined with worry. "Larry, have you been in here yet this morning?"

"No, sir. I opened Mr. Phillips' door and was just about to open Mrs. Montes' door when I saw it was already open," I said, with a questioning look on my face.

"Well, I don't know what's going on. Maybe I need to take a day off. I came down the hall this morning, and I heard shuffling going on in here like a squirrel loose on the teacher's desk or something. I opened the door and saw all these papers on the floor, and some were still just lighting down, like I caught someone messing with her desk mid-stream but, Larry, there was no one in here. I got this cold chill up my spine, and I declare, Larry, it felt like there was a presence in this room. Like someone was in here with me." He sat down in the teacher's chair and heaved a heavy sigh. "Do you think I've lost it, Mr. Rodriguez?"

Now he never called me "Mr. Rodriguez." I don't mean like he disrespected me or anything, but we relate to one another as boss and employee, so I knew he was really shaken.

"Mr. McCrank," I said, "I had some weird things happen to me, and I heard weird things yesterday. I came down to the office to talk to you about it, but you were in the cafeteria and then busy with other school business. I had decided this morning to just let it go. Get a fresh start, but I guess I am not going to be able to do that. I don't guess we have time to talk about all of it right now. If it's okay with you, I will just clean up these papers, and maybe you and I can talk after school. I'd say during lunch, but I know how in demand you are. Will that be okay?" I know I had just taken the lead there, which was out of place, to say the least, but he looked like a man who needed a jump start.

"Yeah, yeah, sure. We will definitely take some time to talk about it after school. Hopefully, nothing else wild happens during the meantime. I was supposed to be in the gym to monitor a girls' volleyball game, but I'll see if I can get Mrs. Nunez to cover. Thanks, Larry. I'll see you then."

With that, he was out the door. His calling me "Larry" as he left gave me a sense of comfort. Sort of told me that he had regained his composure a little. Old Mr. McCrank. He spent a lot of time in the Navy. No telling what he might have seen out there on the open seas. I know that not all Navy men spend their time on the open sea, but Mr. McCrank did. He was on some ship; he has told me which one before, but I can't remember which one, several years of his military career. He really loved the Navy. Told me I should persuade any kid that was thinking about a military career to think about the Navy. I know that his view was somewhat skewed based on his experience, but it was still one worth considering.

As Mr. McCrank headed out of the room, it was sort of like he was levitating. It was weird. I got down on my knees to pick up the papers. What in the world was going on? "God," I said, "I know that there is some kind of spiritual energy in this room. I know that none of this has escaped your notice. I know that your power is greater than any spirit because all spirits come from you, and all spirits eventually return to you. You created us all. Father, could this be the spirit of that little girl that was killed here all those years ago? If so, why is she still here? What needs to happen to free her of this place so that she can join that 'Great cloud of witnesses' the book of Hebrews talks about? Somehow, I get this feeling that you want me to help her with this, but that can't be right, can it? I am a school janitor. I have no theological degrees or special calling. Nevertheless, Father, I am your servant. Do with me what you think is right and in Jesus' name, help this girl find peace."

I ended my prayer, now having the papers back in order and on Mrs. Montes' desk. I headed out to make sure there were plenty of hand towels and toilet paper in all the bathrooms. I gave a look back as I left the room. What is going on in here? What is going on in this school? For that matter, what is going on in my life? Am I somehow caught up in this? I sure didn't want to be. You know, I say that, but at the same time, the little voice inside of me says, "Yes, but isn't it exciting? Don't you want to get to the bottom of it? Should you maybe even feel a little honored to be on the inside for once instead of on the outside looking in?" Sometimes that little voice makes me think I might be a bit unbalanced. If somehow, I could step out of this situation and view it as a third party, one that is not right in the middle of the mess but as an analytical observer. Maybe I could make something of it.

As the day progressed, everything went along as it usually does. The bell rang, and the kids came in, dragging desert sand and leaves in on my clean floors as per normal. The speaker came on the intercom system, and all the students stood for the Pledge of Allegiance and then a moment of silence. Next came the announcements. Don't forget the football game on Thursday evening at five pm against Vista. The cheerleaders will be selling face paintings during lunch of the school's mascot, the cougar. The normal stuff. I saw a kid or two scurrying into their classrooms late, excuses in hand.

I headed on down to the teacher's lounge. It forms a long rectangle with doors on either end. Down at one end is a small kitchen, complete with microwave and refrigerator, not to mention cabinets where various supplies are kept. You know the sort: salt and pepper, paper plates, coffee cups, creamer, etc. In that main rectangle of the lounge, there are folding tables and another refrigerator, and two or three microwaves. There may not be anyone in the lounge most of the day, but when a teacher has to grab their lunch and rush to the lounge to heat it up, you sure don't want them waiting in line. It can get dicey, let's say. Anyway, on the other end of the rectangle is a small office where teachers can go to make calls home to parents. It is very small, maybe six feet by six feet, so no one hangs out in there. It's a business-only kind of room. There is a door out into the courtyard down on this end. In the courtyard are a couple of tables for teachers to go out and have their lunch if they like on nice days. In the courtyard, there are flower beds that the gardening club maintains, and there are several non-fruit-bearing mulberry trees to offer much-needed shade from the hot New Mexico sun. While this is not needed very much in the bliss of October, come spring, that shade will be much welcomed. There are double doors on the other side of the courtyard that lead back to the front office. This is an old school, over fifty years old, yet there is a rightness about the way it was laid out. It's like you can feel the desire the men and women of so long ago had for making this a haven for learning.

Back in the lounge, I clean up the coffee spills by the coffee maker and the various grounds and crumbs left by teachers on the move. I pour myself a cup of coffee and sit down at one of the tables. The steam rising up off the black coffee calmed my spirit somehow. I love the way it seems to move with no apparent influences. It just floats and sways. Peaceful. Reluctantly, I leave my refuge and get on with my day. Out in the hall, I see Ms. David heading purposely toward a classroom. Even in her busyness, she takes time to look up and smile.

"Hey, Mr. Rodriguez, how are you doing today?" She asks.

"Just fine, Ms. David. Nice to see you." I return her smile.

"The floors look great, Larry. You make us proud," she says, offering her hand for a high five. My hand rises to meet hers. We slap hands, and she hurries off to look after the school that is her life. Her devotion to this school inspires us to want more from ourselves and these kids. She makes us believe that despite many of these kids' circumstances, they can be raised up to make this a better world. God's own hand creates people like Cathy David. May she feel his pleasure.

And, you know, she doesn't have to do that. She's a busy lady with all kinds of responsibilities as the principal of the school, but she looks up and sees people and makes them feel like they are part of something good. The way she dresses also tells me that she is not about herself. She dresses fine, but she is not dressed to the nines, making herself a showpiece day after day. She dresses to work and to relate to those who also have come to lay it on the line to make this place as good as any. She is the primary reason the culture of this school is positive in an area of town that could be seen as a ghetto. Lots of people here are working to make this school a better place, but I believe that it is Ms. David that has turned the ship and taken this school from one better left unmentioned to one in which I can say I am proud I work. Most of the kids and teachers and others that spend time here want to be here. That's saying a lot about the way things are these days. It seems to me that most folks are just trying to make it through another day, let alone live it with joy and purpose. Maybe all of us should open our ears and eyes and see what purpose God is seeking to wield through us. Our lives might not be easier, but wouldn't they be much richer?

When Jesus is telling his parable in the New Testament, he often says something like, "He who has ears to hear, let him hear." Or he condemns people for having eyes but still not seeing. Ms. David sees people. And when they voice concerns, at least from my perspective, she has ears to hear. There is a lot of hardness in the world. There are so many things that happen that make me wonder why we continue to even try to make it happen sometimes, but when someone wants to, it is just a simple smile or kind word that can make all that dreariness melt away, if only for a short while. And it costs them nothing except awareness of the power of influence they yield. I do not know why God has chosen to open my mind to these things, but I praise Him for the grace of seeing the beauty he has so bountifully splashed around me, seemingly, just for my enjoyment. "Thank you, Father. Thank you," I say in a whisper.

Down at my janitor's closet, I stop and get a couple of trash bags. I need to go scour the campus, and especially along the chain link fence, for trash. Out in the desert, the wind blows. The trash from blocks away becomes yours in moments, especially if one of those dust devils comes along. They really are like mini tornadoes. They pick things up here and deposit them there. After last night's wind gusts, I am sure I won't be lacking something to do.

As soon as I go outside and adjust to the bright New Mexico sun (if you haven't experienced it, the word glare might help you grasp it), I see the trash trapped on the chain link fence like a coffee filter catches the grounds. So much trash! At least the fence gives me a good collection point. Three and a half bags of trash have been gathered, stuffed down, and packed together when I take a breather. I stuff them down well and tight, packing the trash in so I can make the most of my efforts. The gym kids are out playing kickball. I always loved playing that game. It doesn't require the equipment of other sports, so any group of kids can play if they can find something to serve as bases and a ball. I'll never forget that time Dean, a buddy of mine, ran up to kick the ball and the whole sole of his tennis shoe ripped off. Everybody laughed, even Dean. The teacher found some duct tape and taped his shoe up so he could make it through the day. Those old Converse, everybody wore them back then, would begin to wear at the toe, and then your toes would start poking out of them if you kicked something wrong with your toe. And they would wear a hole over on the insole where these two breather holes were. Eventually, what happened to Dean's shoes was the fate of all converse tennis shoes, unless you were fortunate enough to get new shoes before that happened. Today it seems there are thrift stores everywhere, and you can get some pretty good clothes or shoes there if you need them. I don't remember thrift stores from when I was growing up. Maybe they were around, but I grew up in a pretty small border town, so they may not have been available to us back then.

I saw a little boy; He was surely a sixth grader; he was so small, taking his turn at kicking the ball. The pitcher rolled the ball into home plate, and the little guy gave it his best whack. It went over toward third base. The baseman rushed in and picked up the ball to throw to first, but the speedy little guy was already rounding first and on second base before they got control of the ball again. He was smiling, fit to kill. The others were shaking their heads. "Rodriguez, man, you are fast!" One of the boys said. "Racing Rodriguez is more like it," another said. The boy, no bigger than a mite, loved the praise. The pitcher got the ball back and rolled it into the next batter. The kid, Rodriguez, was now back to his game face as he prepared to race to third on contact. "Those Rodriguez', you know. What can I say?" It was only later that I made the connection of who this kid was.

Chapter 9

Picking up trash is sort of therapeutic for me. I know that sounds weird, but making my world (which is almost completely made up of this little school in this medium-sized town in a state that many people in America don't seem to know, is a state of its own and not still part of Mexico), better, that's my mission. Cleaning up the trash one section at a time is like waging a systematic war in which I can actually see progress. If the results of a clean campus only last for a day, then at least I have that temporary victory. Many people, it seems to me, live their lives like they haven't had a victory in recent memory. The Apostle Paul writes, "Do you not know that in a race all compete, but only one receives the prize? Run in such a way that you may win it." That's the way I want to live my life. My relationship with Jesus Christ gives me the daily power to do it. To live victoriously, even as a janitor. Again, from Paul, "For I am convinced, that neither death nor life, neither angels nor demons, neither the present nor the future, nor any powers, neither height nor depth, nor anything else in all creation, will be able to separate us from the love of God that is in Christ Jesus our Lord." Such words as these drive my day.

In the wind, the flags blow, showing me that the wind is probably blowing around five to seven miles per hour. That's a good day to pick up trash. In the spring, the winds will go thirty or forty miles per hour, even creating brownout times when the only wise thing to do is stay inside with all the windows closed. The sands of Arizona will be happy to find a new home all over your furniture and counters if you don't. This kind of wind is just right to make the flags of the United States and New Mexico dance lightly, showing off their colors.

I love the flag of New Mexico with all its symbolism. Spanish colors of the conquistadors, the Zia symbol, honoring Native Americans, and the different stages and influences on our lives. But "Old Glory," the U.S. flag, is the one that really gets to me. When I think of the places it flies, my heart swells with pride. I've seen them place that flag on the moon. I've been all over this country and seen that no matter where I am, that flag tells me that we are one nation, despite our many differences in culture and opinion. So, when I stand up during the Pledge of Allegiance, my devotion is to all those who have made my freedom possible. I have had many people in my family commit years of their lives to protect this country, and I know so many more that would stand shoulder to shoulder to protect her still today. God bless America! God bless America! I love her so much. I love that red and yellow flag that flies out front of our school, remembering that it is represented by one of those white stars on our nation's flag. The seasons of the year, the times of the day, the stages of life, and the directions of the compass. The Zia symbol is a spiritual symbol. If we take time to reflect on these things, we will live deeper, richer lives. I believe that. As I get older, the stages of life have much more meaning to me. I am not yet in the autumn of my life, but I've certainly come to the point of considering my days much more than when I was young. My eyes see more, and my mind comprehends more. It may be this very thing that is allowing Mr. McCrank and me to see and experience these apparently spiritual happenings at our school. Not all activity in the spiritual realm is angels and hope for a brighter future. According to the Bible, Satan is the ruler of the power of the air, the spirit that is now at work among those who are disobedient, Ephesians 2:2. Those who are in Christ have spiritual armor to protect them against the darkness (of evil) 1 Thessalonians 5:4-11. Well, I don't know all the verses about it, but I learned enough growing up that even the Bible teaches that there are some things going on around us that most of us aren't even aware of. I keep a little pocket New Testament with me that I read as a reference most days. It helps me keep things in a proper perspective.

O, well, I guess I kind of got lost in my thoughts there for a minute. I grabbed my trash bags and headed over to the dumpster, and tossed them inside. The dumpsters are over on the north side of the cafeteria. Now that I think about it, it might be a good idea to move them away from the windows of the cafeteria. Not the best view from the dining room, but I guess they have been here for years and are not likely to be moved now. I notice that the recycle bins are completely full and am glad that today is the scheduled day for its pick up. Our school and our town have really gotten on board with recycling. "Reduce, Reuse, Recycle." My old Abuela would have surely loved that. People in her day saved everything and reused every glass jar for canning, every paper bag for gathering vegetables for giving away to neighbors. They were recycling before recycling was cool. With these thoughts in my mind, I head back inside. The bell would be ringing before I knew it, and they would need me to help direct traffic. Where our school is, several teachers, administrators, and I get to help direct buses, kids, or through traffic once the bell rings. It's an okay assignment. It gives me a chance to speak to the kids as they are leaving or even see some of the students who went to school here in the past as they come in to get their little brothers or sisters or even, in some cases, their own children. Hard to believe I am old enough to have those experiences. And then again, not really. The clock is ticking.

The temperature has warmed up now, and I am out only in my long sleeve work shirt. Janitors wear these light blue work shirts that button up along the front. They have pockets on the breast with those little flaps on them and a place for a pencil. I have always loved them. I don't ever want to wear a shirt without pockets, and I don't care for polo shirts. Give me my work shirt any day. My black hair blows in the breeze as I direct the traffic. I'm in my fifties now, but the heritage God has given me will allow my hair to keep its color for years to come. I love that part of who I am. I see Josh Trujillo and call out to him as he pulls in to pick up his kids. "Hey, Larry. How's it going?" He says.

"Good, good, Josh. Hey, your kids are growing up fast. They are looking good," I say as he pulls forward. Each car is inching forward as so many are picking up their kids. It's hard to believe that Josh is old enough to have three kids in our school now. He was in school here when I first started working as a janitor. For some reason, he and I kind of took up with each other back then. I kept up with his sports, even through high school. He was a fine running back over at La Plata High and not a bad baseball player. Good kid. Now, look at him. Sort of like me, I think. He came from a poor family, his dad long gone. His mom work two jobs, and his grandmother basically doing the raising of him and his brother and two sisters. A poor boy did well. I see him every now and then up at Home Depot. He is one of the managers there. I am so proud of him. It really doesn't matter so much which cards you are dealt. What matters is what you do with them once they are in your hands.

When the cars had all pulled through, and the kids were all picked up, for the most part, I picked up the cones we placed out in the school drive to help direct the parent pick up and put them in the janitor's closet. There are always kids that are picked up late, either because their parents are late getting there or, most often, because they are involved in an after-school club or sport. This facility gets used. It certainly was not built to gather dust. I had headed inside, and I was just getting started with my sweep of the classrooms, picking up the daily trash, when I saw Mr. McCrank coming toward me. He was older than me, the maybe late fifties or even sixty, but somehow, he had the boundless energy required of someone who serves as an administrator of a middle school.

"How did the day go, Larry? It's been so busy today I've hardly had time to look up and see anybody." As he says this, he gives me that crusty little Navy smile of his.

"O, today was another good one, Mr. McCrank," I say, leaning my dust mop against the dry erase board. "No one got sick and threw up, so that puts it in the good category right there. I didn't hear about any fights, so that gives it another good mark," I say. "I spent quite a bit of time picking up the trash that the winds blew in last night and got to watch the kids out playing kickball. Add that to my regular rounds, and, well, let's just say, I didn't get bored. How about you? You had a pretty busy day, huh?"

"Yeah, yeah. You know, meetings with new students' parents, and we had to meet with the team leaders about the holidays, how all that was going to play out. It's all good, though."

I could see he was about to adjust the direction of our conversation.

"Hey, Larry, have you seen or heard anything else strange since we talked the other morning in Ms. Montes' classroom?" He asked. He fidgeted a bit when he did, like he had something he wanted to tell me but wanted to get my feedback first.

"Well, now. I was hoping to get to talk to you. That was this morning, Mr. McCrank. Remember? That sure was a mess of papers on the floor. I guess it all kind of runs together for me too. So much going on. I have heard some other tales from teachers, just at random talking. I was just cleaning up like I always do. I certainly didn't lead the conversations. Plus, I had a bit of a weird experience all my own, but that could have just been me getting a little carried away with all this spooky business, I don't know," I responded.

"What kind of things? Just silly stuff, you think? He asked.

"Mmm, probably. I mean, Mr. Rigsby was saying the T.V. in Mr. Jackson's room sort of came on by itself, and it was all snowy, and then there was this image of a girl with messed up hair, and then it went off. And then Mrs. Douglass mentioned about books in her poetry section being off on the floor every morning, and then I had this weird experience with some white flowers, and then several ghosts' songs came on my truck radio as that was going on. Probably all just coincidence, but it sure had me freaked out for a while. It's all very strange, but there has to be some rational explanation. Please don't tell anybody else what I just told you. I don't want folks to think I'm a freak or something," I told Mr. McCrank.

"Whoa, now. You are going to have to break all that down for me. Listen, Larry, we are going to have to get to the bottom of this. I have been here several years, and I have heard some things, and some things have happened to make me wonder, but never this many things all at once. It's starting to creep me out. Last night I was over in the gym for a volleyball game. I had to supervise the activity and make sure everyone left when the games were over," He took a breath.

I took the opportunity to ask him how we did.

"O, the girls had a rough start this year, but both our A and B teams won last night. We were playing Sierra, and they are not a bad team, but our girls looked like they were beginning to click, you know what I mean? Anyway, I made sure to tell Coach Jensen that they were looking good. She said, sort of under her breath, "Thanks. It's about time. I was beginning to wonder."

I laughed and said, "Yeah, that sounds like Coach Jensen. She has put some really good teams together in the past. Sounds like she has finally got these girls going in the right direction too. Thanks, Mr. McCrank. I appreciate the update. I have been working late in the building cleaning up lately because Jose and Martin have both been out with some sort of virus. By the time I get over to the gym, it's all over with. Anyway, sorry. I interrupted you," I said.

"That's okay, Larry. Like I was saying, when I went to lock up, I heard something back in the gym. I went in to locate the source of the noise. After a minute, I could tell it was coming from under the bleachers on the home side. I figured surely some of those kids were still hanging out. I hadn't put the bleachers in like we do after a game because we have that pep rally tomorrow for the football team. When I went back to the bleachers, I heard it again. It was a kid, even a young girl's moan, and when I looked, high and low, I saw no one. I went out and checked the visitor's side. Nothing. I went back and checked the home side one more time. Nothing. I hung around a little while after that, kind of creeped out, but then I got a text from my wife asking where I was and could I pick up some bread on the way home. So, I stopped by Albertsons and grabbed the bread and a gallon of milk, and some oats. I always eat oats for breakfast, and besides, I can never go to the grocery store and just get what I came for.

When I was coming out of the store, I saw this girl over by the cart return. She was looking at me with the strangest look. I normally don't pay much attention to people at the store. I'm all business, you know. I was tired and just wanted to get home, but this girl...." He paused, and his gaze was as if he was looking at something far away.

"What did she look like, Mr. McCrank? I asked.

"Well," He began. "She was young. I'd say around thirteen years old. She had dark, dark hair. Of that part, I am sure. Her hair was almost blue; it was so dark, if you know what I mean. And her eyes, it seemed like they jumped out at me. I'm sure they were just normal size, but there was something about them that caught me. I don't know. It's all so far out. That's funny. I haven't used that phrase in half of my forever. But I do think that best describes it."

"Mr. McCrank, what was it about the eyes…I mean, what color were they, and what caused them to stand out like that? I asked. He really had my attention now, and I was hanging on every word he said.

"Larry, her eyes weren't brown like so many who go to school here, or blue or even green. They were some kind of golden mosaic…beautiful really, but almost pleading eyes. Maybe pleading is not the right word. Let me just say, they begged my attention, and then…." He trailed off and looked back around the room like he was hunting for something.

"Then what, Mr. McCrank? Did she speak to you?" I asked.

"No, no, Larry, she didn't say a word. Her image just faded away. I stood there a minute, and then I rubbed my eyes and looked again. Nothing there. I wasn't afraid, Larry, I wasn't afraid at all, but my curiosity and, I guess I'll call it yearning, was just not willing to let it alone. I want to know what's going on, Larry. I feel like this girl; this ghost girl is not trying to be a menace or scare anyone; I think she is trying to find something or resolve something. I think she was crying out to me for help with that look of hers. Who am I, Larry? I don't know anything about the spirit world or ghosts or anything. Till all this happened to me, if you had told me what I just told you, I might not laugh at you in the face, but I'd think you were off your rocker. I might even see about replacing you with someone more "safe" for the kids to be around. What's happening to me, Larry? Am I losing my mind?" He asked. He ruffled his thinning hair, looking at me imploringly.

I wanted to be really careful how I responded to Mr. McCrank. He was as super confused as was I. He and I had worked together for a long time, and since we both came in early, we spent quite a bit of time together in the mornings over the years and after school at ballgames and other school functions, but he had never confided with me like this before.

"Mmm, Mr. McCrank, there have been a lot of crazy things going on. Several people are talking about it, so you are not alone in this. I think I told you about my crazy experience going home the other night after I got off from work. So, you're not the only one." I said, hoping to make him feel better. The girl you just described sounds like the girl Mr. Rigsby saw on the T.V. screen.

Dark hair. All messed up. Young, maybe thirteen, he told me, just like you said. This can't be a coincidence, Mr. McCrank."

"Very interesting. Hmm." He sighed and then said, "Mr. Rodriguez, we have been talking awhile, and both of us have things to do to get ready for tomorrow. Will you have time to talk later, before you go home? I don't think you told me about what happened the other night, but I am interested in hearing about it." He was back to being the vice-principal. Responsibilities, duties, and other concerns. I guess that's what makes him a good leader. His ability to just disengage with one thing and focus all his attention elsewhere immediately like that. He must have learned that skill in the Navy.

"Sure," I said. "I should be finished with my duties by six thirty or so if I hurry. I'd like to get this off my chest."

About the time I told Mr. McCrank I'd be finished, I remembered that I told Rosa that I would try to hurry home tonight. I hated to put Mr. McCrank off, but my Rosa would be waiting. We were both in our fifties, but our love for each other was just as alive as it was when we were in our twenties, if possible, maybe even more.

I saw Mr. McCrank in his office. He was also our athletic director, so he was responsible for scheduling games and officials, getting someone to work for the scoreboard, etc. Too much for me to get my head around. It looked like he was going over a schedule when I walked in.

"Hey, Larry," he said, looking up. "I had forgotten about this scheduling conflict for our next volleyball game. The girls at Picacho had a death in one of the girl's families, and the services for the girl were scheduled on the same night we were supposed to play. I am trying to find a different day for us to play. It's going to take a while. I guess we'll have to talk tomorrow sometime."

"That's fine, Mr. McCrank. I was just coming up to tell you that I remembered I told my wife I'd try to get home earlier tonight, so this sort of works out for me. I didn't want to put you off. Sorry, you have to work so hard, though," I said.

"Good. Go home and enjoy that wife of yours. If a man has a good woman, he ought not to keep her waiting," He said.

"Thanks, Mr. McCrank. I'll see you in the morning. Have a good night, sir," I said and headed out the door. His head was already back in the books, trying to pull a rabbit out of the hat.

When I got home, Rosa had the outdoor light on for me, as she usually does on these short fall days. I really love the long days of summer. Coming home in the dark makes me always feel like I ought to get straight to bed. Crazy how our bodies respond to something as simple as natural light. Still, seeing the home lights on for me made me smile. I couldn't wait to get inside to see my

Rosa. I entered the house to the aroma of chicken fajitas. It caught me, and for a moment, I simply basked in the pleasure of it. Mercy, what a treasure the sense of smell was in a moment like this. I opened my eyes, and Rosa stood there before me. She was dressed in a Mexican fiesta dress, white with green and orange laced through the trim. Her dark brown hair was up in a bun. She was smiling at me. She came forward and took my hand, pressing a button on her phone that played some of the traditional Mexican music from when we were young. We danced. Right there in the kitchen and dining room area, like we were in some fancy dance hall. She was so beautiful I could not take my eyes off her. How could I be married to this beautiful woman? Mercy, Lord. Mercy!

Without going into any details, we had to reheat the fajita sometime later. We sat there at the table, just loving being in one another's presence. Looking at me with her beautiful brown eyes, she said, "Larry, I wanted to explain about the flowers last night. Dia de los Muertos is coming in just a few days. When I was a little girl, we always held this holiday in high honor. As you know, we joined our relatives who had passed in eating and drinking and dancing together. We would tell stories of those who had gone on before and talk to them as if they were sitting there with us. You know how it is. Anyway, we also had this tradition that if someone in our family was nearing their time of passing on to join them, we brought them a bouquet of white roses. It was a send-off to them as they joined the family on the other side. Well, as you know, my sister, Maria, has been sick off and on. I have been praying for her and have lit a candle for her many times. I guess with the holiday so near and my sister Maria on my mind and then the white roses, I just thought…" she broke off and wiped tears from her eyes. I thought you had news from the family."

O, Honey, I am so sorry. I didn't even think about all that. Sometimes I don't think at all!" I said, disgusted with myself.

"No, No, Baby. I don't want you to feel bad. I just wanted to explain my expression. I know it caught you off guard, and I am sorry. I realized almost immediately that I had made the wrong connection, but a bit too late to keep me from ruining your intentions toward me. I'm sorry, Larry," she said.

"Thanks for explaining, I wasn't sure what it was all about, but now I feel much better. You certainly have made up for it," I said, winking at her.

"She smiled at me and kissed me. "It really has been a special night, hasn't it?" She said, kissing my hands. "How is it possible that we have been married over thirty years and love each other like this?" She asked.

"I'm not sure, Sweetheart," I said, "but bring it on!" Needless to say, we had a very nice evening together.

The next morning, I moved along quickly after I got to school. I left a few things undone in my hurry to get home, so now it was time to make up for it. I hustled to make sure there was plenty of toilet paper and hand towels in all the bathrooms. I also unlocked all the doors for subs that would be in the building today. Because we have a rock star for a principal that knows how to maintain discipline, we have no problem getting substitutes, even on late notice. Some of the schools, I'm told by other janitors in the district, are run like zoos out of control. They can't beg knowing subs to come to those places to fill in. They have to use their educational assistants and even office staff to cover classes. I even heard of one school where the janitor was asked to cover until the sub came. Turned out that the sub never did get there. The janitor kind of felt like he got snowed. No doubt. There is no way I would do that. I'd be like, "I'm out of here," and they wouldn't even see my backside leaving the building; I'd be out of there so quickly.

So many of those in leadership positions in schools wring their hands and trying to figure out how to handle the kids of today. Ms. David, our principal, has it figured out if they would just look at her example. Set the standard and then hold the kids to it. It works. Those who don't meet the standard are punished in one form or another. That also is a key point. She lets the punishment meet the crime. She knows the students, so she is able to do what needs to be done to bring them into compliance. It seems like some principals are afraid to exercise the authority they have. It's like the tail wags the dog. While on the front end, the methods Ms. David uses are not well received by everyone, in the long run, it makes this school tick and has people who live in other middle school areas asking to have their kids transferred to Lynn. I believe that all kids want parameters. It gives them the security they need and want in order to excel in the educational process. Of course, I am just a school janitor, but that is what these eyes see, and my years of living and experience in the school system have shown me. Take it for what it is worth.

Chapter 10

The day went along fine or at least as normal. There are always teachers needing supplies or cleanup, and that's especially true in the cafeteria. There are some kids that just have klutz embedded in their DNA. Thankfully, the kids are required to help clean up any mess they create (this prevents too many "accidents"), but still, the mops need to be brought out or the broom and dust pan. You know, overall, I don't mind it. I like to work, and most of the time, I am just talking to the kids and finding out what's going on with them on their sports team or in the band or where they've gone or are going on field trips. We have a good school where most of the staff and students just see me as another person in the school. They don't feel the need to look down on me or make me their personal servant or anything like that. I saw that little Rodriguez boy headed down the sidewalk from the cafeteria to the sixth-grade hall. He was messing around with a couple of his other buddies, all sixth graders, I figured. "Hey, there's that 'Racing Rodriguez' kid," I called out. He looked up at me and smiled. He was so small and his smile so big it was sort of comical.

"Hey, Larry," He called back to me as he hustled inside. I have never met him, officially, but all the kids know me as 'Larry' around here. I think I'm going to like that kid. I headed on into the cafeteria to clean up after the kids' morning breakfast. Thankfully, at this school, any kid can come in and have breakfast. They don't have to have money. I am not big on big government or the government carrying everyone, but I am glad that our city has seen fit to provide the funds to make sure any kid can come and get breakfast without worrying about how they are going to pay for it. It is mighty hard to concentrate on Language Arts if your stomach keeps interrupting.

When I finished in the cafeteria, I went into the teacher's lounge to do any cleaning up that might need to be done after the teachers and have myself a cup of coffee. We usually have this Folgers Breakfast Blend we brew in this big twenty-cup coffee maker. Man, I love that stuff. It's smooth, you know. Not too bitter. I guess I drink too much of it. Anyway, when I went in one door, there was Mrs. Douglass coming in the other. She had popped in there to get a cup of coffee between the classes that were coming into the library.

"How's it going, Larry?" She asked.

"Fine, fine, Mrs. Douglass. You look fresh today. Did you get your hair done?" I asked.

"I'm just wearing it down today, Larry. I didn't have time to curl it like I usually do. Our baby was awake much of the night with an earache. Poor thing. My husband took the morning off to take her to the doctor. I know it's just the pollen in the air. You know it doesn't take much and, at least for our family, it seems to always be allergy season. We're afraid we might have to get tubes in her ears as we've done with a couple of our other children. But, thanks for the compliment. I'm glad to know that wearing my hair down gives me a fresh look, even if I didn't sleep much." She said with a bit of a sigh.

"O, ma'am, I'm sorry you didn't sleep well. I hope your baby gets well soon. If the baby doesn't sleep well, momma doesn't sleep well. Poor thing." I said.

"Who me, or the baby?" She said back with a grin.

"However it applies, ma'am," I said. I know better than to get in too deep in conversations like this one. "Hey, Mrs. Douglass, I know you need to get back into the library, but are you still having trouble with those poetry books, or did that problem go away? I meant to get in there this morning to check, but I got caught up in other activities." I watched her face. She turned her eyes to mine and gave me the strangest look. There is something about her eyes that I have not seen before. They have a golden mosaic look to them, and her expression made me take a step back.

"Larry, umm, the books in the library are all just fine. Poetry books included."

"Oh, Well, I mean, none of them were knocked off in the poetry section when you came in this morning," I tried again, fiddling with the pen in my shirt pocket, suddenly wishing that I had not brought it up.

"Umm, no, Larry. Everything is like it should be. Thanks for asking?" She ended her comment with a question and looked at me with a look I can't quite describe. It was somehow a look of confusion but also of warning, maybe? I'm just not sure. Crazy things are happening around here. "Okay then," I said. "Let me know if you need anything," I said, excusing myself and heading out of the lounge. Had I just imagined our conversation the other day? Was I beginning to lose touch with reality or something? I mean, this last little conversation had me reeling a bit. I was looking down at the floor, willing books to be there in my mind, but there was nothing. Maybe I had dreamed it all up. Looking up, I saw Mrs. Douglass heading down the hall the other way and into the library. She had gone about her business; it was time for me to do the same. Still, the way she was looking at me with those eyes. They were unusual to begin with, sort of that golden mosaic, as I tried to describe before, but now it was like they had become laser beams. She had left it like that. I guess I was waiting for her to say something like, "Just messing with you, Larry." But she didn't. I don't think she remembered the books being on the floor at all if her expression was any indication. But that can't be right. She told me before that they had been on the floor several times. Not just the one time. Did I imagine all that, and if so, why?

I had other business. I couldn't fry my mind trying to figure out the mind of a woman. Even with my own wife, with whom I had been over thirty years, I still come away scratching my head sometimes. Yes, sir. Back to business that I do understand. Mrs. Morales wants me to bring another desk to her classroom. She's getting another new student. You know how it is this time of year. Something was definitely going on around here, I don't care what you say, but as of now, I don't have a clue what it is.

Out in the hall, I moved quickly on the square tiles that I spent so much time waxing and buffing on off days and sweeping every day, several times a day, especially in the windy spring season when the sands of Arizona seem to blow straight through on their way to Texas. I found the desk down in storage and put it on a cart to take up to Mrs. Morales' room. It seemed to me that there were almost always kids coming and going, in some level of transition. We weren't exactly a military town, but we were less than forty miles from Fort Bliss in Texas, and the Small Missile Range was just across the Organ Mountains, maybe twenty-five miles away. Then, of course, the University was a research center where internationals were always coming to study. All this is not to mention the illegal immigration that repeatedly came up through our southern border. So many of the kids here went back to Mexico over the weekend to see their families. Somehow, someday, someone is going to make migration into this country easier, and for those who just want to come and work during the seasonal harvests and then go home, they will make it where it's not such a big deal. What we could agree on in principle becomes so discombobulated when government red tape gets involved.

Most of my extended family live in Mexico. They are not bad people, but sometimes they do come here without going through the proper channels. I go "home" two or three times a year. I would go more often if I could, but with work and the home here, it's really not practical. But my family is growing older. My grandparents are already dead on my father's side. Only my mother's mother remains alive. We see her every year, making it a point to hold on to that connection. It is doubly important since my mother and father were killed five years ago now in a rollover during one of those freak February ice and snow storms. You know, it seems like winter is over, everybody makes their plans, and then, when unexpected, this storm hits as they are traveling that short road from Palomas to La Plata. How I ache to this day knowing that they died coming up to see us. "O, Mama! O, Papa!" How I miss them. Still, I thank God I have a couple of brothers, Fernie and Chewy, and one sister, Gabby, and their children remaining in Mexico. Mostly around the Palomas area. Sometimes they come up to visit. We try to do things the legal way most of the time. We had some real trouble once when my cousin, Pancho, came up without going through the proper channels. He had gotten into some trouble for fighting on the job. He was arrested for hitting his supervisor. I know it all sounds bad, but his supervisor had pushed this old man who worked in the plant, knocking him to the floor, just because he wasn't working fast enough to please him. I guess he was trying to use the old man as an example to all of them of what would happen if they didn't pull their weight.

Either they would get pushed around or pushed out. Unions were forbidden in the plant. A person would get fired if he just mentioned getting a union to defend the rights of the workers. Pancho, when he saw the old man on the floor, couldn't control himself. He punched his supervisor right in the mouth. It cost him his job and thirty days in jail and also made it nearly impossible for him to cross the border to the United States. I remember asking Pancho what he was thinking. He said, "Lorenzo (that's my real name), when I saw that man push the old guy down; it was like seeing my life pass before me. So many times, I have seen people shoving our people or me down. I just blew it. I'd do it again, bro. I know I would. If we don't speak up for ourselves, if we don't advocate for our people, I don't see anyone else in line to do it for us. Yeah, it messed my opportunity in the U.S. up, but it was still the right thing to do. I'd do it again."

That's why I have helped him come up into the United States. Several times now. He comes to work the chile fields in Hatch and Dona Ana County. He works, sends money home, and when the work is done, he goes home. He doesn't hurt anything. He is a noble man, and I'm glad to possibly bring trouble on myself in order to help him. That's what family does.

I admit some of those who come up from Mexico and other Central and South American countries are coming for a free ride or getting involved in the gangs that have been established along the southern border. And, of course, there is a continual stream of people bringing drugs into this country. They will use any avenue they can find. Secret compartments in vehicles, underground tunnels, breaching border fences, and some have even gone so far as implanting drugs inside people's bodies. I'll spare you the details. It's disgusting. The love of money is the root of all kinds of evil, the Bible says. It sure nailed that one. I believe as long as there are people, there will be great varieties in motivations. Some are noble; some are vile. I cannot speak for them all, but I will speak up for my cousin Pancho.

When I entered Mrs. Morales' classroom, she already had her homeroom students in her classroom. She has about twenty-five students, most of whom are of Hispanic origins. The new little girl is standing by her desk. She is small, with a dark complexion. Her hair was as dark as night, and her eyes brown as the mud around the arroyos here. She is petit. Though she is in seventh grade, she can't weigh more than a sack of dog food. Her face is turned toward me as I bring the desk in.

"Your desk has arrived, Maria. Mr. Rodriguez, will you just put the desk up here by my desk for now. There. Thank you, sir," She said.

She turned to the little girl Maria as I retreated from the room. "See Maria. I told you Larry would bring you a desk right away. We'll just leave your desk here for today until I can work out a new seating arrangement."

The little girl watched me closely as I placed the desk by Mrs. Morales' desk. Like so many, she bore the simple beauty of my people. There was a history in her facial expression that made me feel I could write her story myself, though I had never seen this little girl before. Her story seemed to be the same as mine. Those kept down but ever looking for a path upward. I felt I had made headway in my lifetime and silently prayed that she, too, would find that upward path. A path I had found in my ever-deepening relationship with Jesus.

The class was quiet as I walked down the hall. Mrs. Morales kept her class in good order. The homeroom was a time for kids to do homework, turn in paperwork for the office, or read quietly. Mrs. Morales had been teaching for several years and still very much loved her job. She would come early and stay late, not because she was just trying to stay caught up, but to give these kids a learning experience that surpassed what the state expected. That self-driven, high standard is what made and continues to make America a place people will sacrifice to come to. And this little red head of a stepchild school, long replaced by the newer, more technologically savvy schools, is still a model of the can-do spirit that made America great. God bless her. And God bless Patton Middle School.

Wow. Sometimes I sort of go on these little mind trips. I have done almost all of my morning chores when I come back to earth. It's like I live two lives sometimes. The physical one that everybody sees, and this otherworldly existence, like a spiritual journey I'm on, or something. Hey, don't judge me. I guess this job, working as a school janitor, is perfect for me. I don't suppose I should be checking out like this if I were, say, a truck driver. I'd be coming to and see that I was in Seattle or Cleveland. It would be hard to explain that to base, especially if my destination were San Francisco or Cincinnati.

After work, I went home and got cleaned up. I called my wife and asked her if I could take her out to eat at La Posta in Mesilla tonight. She was pleased and readily accepted. We both loved the ambiance of the old restaurant. It has been there since 1939. All kinds of dignitaries and celebrities have eaten there. Even Franklyn Delano Roosevelt had dinner there once, long ago, or at least, so they say. The town of Mesilla is the very place where the Gadsden Purchase was signed in 1852, ceding southern New Mexico and the southern section of present-day Arizona to the United States. Billy, the Kid, was also in jail here once before Pat Garrett put a bullet in him and killed him. Someone put a bullet in Pat Garrett sometime later up on the east side of La Plata, off Highway 70. He who lives by the sword dies by the sword, it is said. I love the history of this area, though much of it is tragic. It's crazy to discover that Mesilla once had a larger population than nearby La Plata. It was, in fact, the base for the Confederate government during the American Civil War in the 1860s. Mesilla is a beautiful town, and it is certainly worth a visit. In fact, it is such a haven that I tried to find a home there for Rosa and me many years ago, but I didn't have two dimes to rub together, and my job at the time would have made it very hard to keep up with a mortgage. We decided instead to make our home in the older part of La Plata, Dona Ana, actually, which is a little north of town. We bought an old adobe home that had seen better days and, over the years, made improvements, bit by bit, until we have a home we are pleased with today. It is still a small and humble home, but we are proud to call it our own and have no desire to leave it. I believe it will be the place where we live out our lives if God wills. Home is where the heart is, it has been said. I believe they got that right. Our lives are wrapped up in the house we've lived in for over thirty years now. I want no other. It is a part of who I am. Nevertheless, I have fond thoughts of Mesilla and am glad to pay it a visit this evening with my beautiful wife, Rosa.

We get dressed up in some of our better clothes. She wears an ankle-length cotton dress, yellow with these little puff balls dangling around the bottom trim, and has puffed sleeves. It is a modest dress, but she looks so beautiful in it, like Mexico itself. With the dress, she wears a necklace of three silver crosses, the symbol of La Plata. Over her shoulders, she wears a shawl, also cotton and solid black. She wears sandals that have flat bottoms and thin black straps. She wears her hair up in a bun, bound with a silver and turquoise hairpin. Myself, I wear my black suit, the one that we were married in all those years ago. I have a string bow tie I wear with it and my black Justin boots that have served me well for many a year. I have them shined up so that they gleam in the light. My hair is slicked back and shining black. We looked good enough to have our picture taken. As we leave our house, I open my truck door for my wife. I reach in and take out a yellow rose boutonniere that I picked for the occasion and pin it on Rosa's black shawl. Honestly, I didn't know that she was going to wear her yellow dress and black shawl, but sometimes it seems like God sheds his favor down on me. It looked perfect on her, and the look in her eyes as I pinned it on her made me feel like we were off to the senior prom. God, sometimes I just feel like shouting, "Yes!" This was definitely one of those moments. We don't go out much and more than that, to us, dinner at La Posta is like going home to Mexico. This was going to be a special night. When you go to La Posta, the ceiling beams come down on you as you walk through the adobe walls. A beautiful senorita in traditional dress leads you to a solid wooden table engraved with birds or flowers. As soon as you sit down, warmed chips and salsa are brought to your table. Drink orders are taken, and menus are given. Your server introduces herself and makes you feel like the place has been reserved for you and yours alone. The salsa is very tasty but not too hot. While traditional Mexican music plays softly in the background, you peruse the menu. I don't think you can miss here, but I recommend the La Posta House Special to newcomers. It is a beautiful meal of tacos, enchiladas, and Chile Rellenos. Before the meal, you get a salad, and after the meal, an empanada with vanilla ice cream. My wife and I shared this meal and then asked for a box to take the rest home. You will love this restaurant. You might have to wait a bit, but it's worth it. They have a couple of little souvenir/jewelry stores just after you go in, so you can use your wait time to see the interesting things they have there and maybe take something home to remember your visit.

When we arrived in Mesilla, we drove through the plaza to see the lights. There is a beautiful Catholic church, Saint Albino's, at the head of the plaza and a wonderful gazebo in the center. The streets are made of brick all the way around the plaza. There are many stores that sell souvenirs and other items crafted by the locals. There are two honey farms in Mesilla, and the honey from these farms will help ward off colds and sinus issues. If you go there at the right (or maybe wrong time), you will find the bees swarming everywhere around you. It is a bit terrifying until you realize that these bees are just about their business and aren't interested in ruining your day. When you finally relax about it, it is really a very cool experience. Anyway, buying this local honey is definitely worth a little more than you would pay in a grocery store for honey packaged out of Missouri or some other place off from here. Many events take place in Mesilla every year. Even now, the plaza is being staged for the Day of the Dead ceremony. Each year families make altars for family members who have passed on. They place photos, mementos, and various flowers or food to welcome their family members back. The ceremony welcomes back those who have passed on once a year. For that time, the living and the dead commune together like old times. This is that "Great cloud of witnesses" that Hebrews 12:1 speaks of. It is a tradition that I love. To think that our ancestors are keeping an eye on us and even are still alive in the presence of God. Jesus himself mentions this when the Sadducees question him about marriage in heaven. He says that before God, all are alive. Luke 20:38. If that is a reality for God, then it is a reality for us. In this way, I know that I am never alone. Rosa and I don't have an altar set up here, but we do have one set up in our backyard. We are not Catholic, but we come from families that were. We love this tradition, and we set out foods and drinks, even little trinkets that remind us of our people. We always put out flowers and light candles in their honor. God forbid that I forget those who have plowed the field before me.

We park in the far lot and walk across the street to the restaurant. The nearby lot is full, but we don't mind the walk. When we enter, we are greeted by a hostess who, to our surprise, is able to usher us straight back to a table rather than put our names on a waiting list. Very nice. We are taken down a hall with low ceilings and around to the left, where we are given a very private table. It's like we are on a date, which I suppose we are. We have been married for decades now, and it seems we are always just together. That spark that we once felt when being brought back into one another's presence has been missing somehow, but tonight, with this table and this restaurant, for this moment, we both feel the tingle of being alone together. I reach across the table and hold her hand. She squeezes mine, and we gaze into one another's eyes. Wow! I really didn't expect this. The waitress hustles up with the chips and salsa and menus. When she sees us, she discerns that this is more than just a dinner engagement. "Pardon, senor, y senora. Can I get you something to drink tonight?" She says, with a twinkle in her eye. "I don't mean to interrupt."

We snap out of our trance and, a bit embarrassed, order our drinks. I know that a lot of people come here for the margaritas, but neither my wife nor I drink. Both of us have experienced family and friends who have simply destroyed their lives with drink, so we have taken a hard right and drink no alcohol at all. So, my wife orders sweet tea, and I decide on water only for tonight. The meal will be delicious enough on its own after we order (we have the fajita meal and share it. The portions are huge, and we save a lot of money that way without all the waste). We fidget around a bit, taking in our surroundings, and then we just start talking. We talk of old times, even back to when we first met. I asked her about her day today and her dreams for our future. She is my wife, and tonight, I am so proud to be here alone with her. She seems to share my heart tonight. My God, How I love this woman! She is the beauty I came courting all those years ago, and tonight I can see that same sweet girl across the table from me.

She is the girl I first saw working the harvest with her family. My family was doing the same in the fields north of us now, in Dona Ana, not far from where we made our home. I remember beginning another hot day of back-breaking work and not being very happy about it. I mean, it was just the routine, and we did what we did, but it was just another day. And then I looked up, stretching my back, and they're just a few rows over from my family was this beautiful girl in a white dress. Like that, all other thoughts were gone, and I was lost. The same girl that caught my eye all those years ago was sitting across from me. It's like there is something magical in this place. I have been here many times before, all of which have been nice, but tonight. Well. This is what memories are made of.

My wife spoke up, breaking the spell or maybe enriching it. "Honey, thank you for bringing me here tonight. I'm not sure why, but I feel almost like a young woman again. Being here with you tonight makes me want this moment to go on and on." Her face beamed as she spoke to me. Call me crazy, but it was as if there was an aurora about her. You have to know that a place like this, in this old Mexican village, has, has to have the ghosts of many who have gone on before swirling about it. Many of them, the best ones, are here with us right now. I don't know how I know, but I do. It's like they are all cheering us on. "Go, Rosa! Go Lorenzo!" they are shouting. You can do this thing. Whatever comes before you, it will be moved aside, and you will live victorious lives in

Jesus' name. My wife is a wonderful woman and very religious. She believes, even more so than myself, that God is involved in every aspect of our lives. Though the mysteries of life are great, it is good to have that assurance and be at peace without being able to explain everything.

"Rosa, I feel it too. You know, it's kind of like Jacob when he woke up that night and realized that angels were ascending and descending from earth to heaven, from heaven to earth. 'This is the doorway to heaven,' he said. 'This is the very house of God.'"

"Exactly, Lorenzo. God is here. In this place with us right now. Why are we so blessed, Lorenzo? What have we done to be honored to be in the presence of the Almighty?" She asked. I know you are not going to believe this, but it felt to me as if we were six feet off the ground. Like we were floating in the air like that crazy scene from Mary Poppins when Bert and the children and Uncle Albert are all singing 'We love to laugh.' Remember that scene. It killed me, and although this is not a comedy scene like that one, it certainly is a scene where my wife and I are just levitating above this restaurant floor with hearts full of joy in one another.

"No, Rosa. But I do know this. The things that have been happening at school are spiritual forces that have somehow awakened, and they need the hand of God to tame them. Remember that scene where Jesus casts out the demons that were in a man who was called Legion? Our God is greater than the most powerful spirits. When we celebrate El Dia de Los Muertos, we celebrate our family but also the God who holds us all together, whether we exist in this world or the next one. Rosa, gracias. Dios, gracias. I feel like a load has been lifted off me. I can go back to school now with the full assurance that whatever is going on there, the power of Almighty God will not back down or bow down to it. Neither will I." I said all this without thinking. I had held back most of the crazy that was going on at school from Rosa. I didn't want to scare her, but now I had let the cat out of the bag.

"Larry, I know you told me some weird stuff was going on at school, but this sounds like more than what I was thinking. Has it gotten worse?" She asked, worry creasing her face.

I could see that I had messed up and gotten into a real kettle of fish. The night had gone so well, and I hated for it to get off track with all the things that were going on at school. It wasn't that I didn't want to tell Rosa all of it and get her ideas on it and have her praying over the situation, but it was so detailed. So complicated. I tried to sort of smooth it out.

"Honey, hmmm, what has been happening at school is, like I just said, it is something that is happening in the spiritual world. I thought it was all just a bunch of coincidences at first, but now I know that we need God to intervene at Patton Middle School. We need for him to take hold of the situation and help bring the spiritual forces under his control and into peace. I will tell you more about it if you want, but for now, I want to ask you to pray over us. You have long been a prayer warrior, and I have seen God use you to break the hold of Satan in many lives. I don't have a good grip on all the details, but I know that none of this has escaped his notice. Let me just say that there is a young girl spirit in our school. She has been trapped there for decades since she was killed accidentally when a janitor named Lee Goodland closed her up in the motorized bleachers after a game one night. As we get closer and closer to Dia de Los Muertos, she has been desperately trying to escape the school and join her family in the Great Beyond to be with that Great Cloud of Witnesses the Bible talks about. For reasons not yet clear to me, it seems that God is using me, among others, especially Mr. McCrank, to help this girl find her peace. Any of us that are outside of God's will for our lives will struggle to find comfort, but God will not give it until we find it by walking in harmony with his Spirit. It is as true for the spiritual world as it is for the physical world. Rosa, I am not sure how I know all this so clearly, but what I have just said is true. I want to help this girl find harmony with God's Spirit so she can go to be with those who have gone on before and so that Patton Middle School will be at peace," I said.

"Larry, I knew that you were having trouble sleeping. With as hard as you work and as many hours as you work, that is not like you. I know you wanted to protect me, but thank you for giving more of the story so I can go into battle with you. You don't need to be fighting this battle on your own," she said.

Chapter 11

The next morning, I got to school early. Time to deal with this situation. I beat Mr. McCrank this time, so I headed straight down the hall to get the coffee going. As I went, I called out to the walls and any spirits that might be in the place, "He is King of kings and Lord of lords! He died to defeat the prince of the ruler of the air, and it is to him that every knee will bow and every tongue confess. Whatever your problem is, he is the answer. Do not resist him, but let him resolve this so you can go to your place of rest. He is the Rock of Ages. All who resist him are crushed, but all who put their trust in him are built up on a foundation that can never be destroyed." When I finished my challenge, I waited for a response. While there was nothing physical that showed itself, I felt a chill come over me, and my spine tingled. I have to admit that for a moment, I was terrified, but then the chill went away, and everything returned to normal. Did that really just happen? I remember this one time when one of the classes went on a field trip to Mesilla. The very place my wife and I visited last night. There was a storyteller that came out to our kids and told them the story of the ghosts that haunted Mesilla and even the age-old story of La Llorona. It really creeped the kids out, one of the teachers told me later. In fact, one of the boys, whose name was Alberto, went down on the ground as the group was leaving the village and claimed that La Llorona was on him, trying to pull him back. Back where, he did not know.

According to the legend, La Llorona became angry with her children and threw them into the Rio Grande River. When she turned to flee the scene of her crime, she caught her foot and fell. Her head struck a rock, and she died. When brought before Saint Peter, she was asked, "Where are your children, La Llorona? Before you can enter these pearly gates, you must bring me your children." From that time until now, La Llorona has gone back and forth on the riverbank of the Rio Grande, calling out, "Mis Hijos. Mis Hijos. Donde son mis Hijos?" Poor Alberto thought maybe she thought she had found one and was dragging him away. I am not sure about Alberto. That whole thing might have just been his imagination or some crazy antics he was pulling to get a girl's attention or something, but the sensation I felt right then. This is real.

In the lounge, I got out the Folgers and got the pot brewing. I left the lounge and went across the hall to unlock the library. I wanted to check on the poetry books. Sure enough, there were six or seven books spread out on the floor. Poe and Shakespeare are among them. "Annabelle Lee" was laid spread open on the floor. "It was many and many a year ago...." I guess that applied to our situation. The poet writes of a love lost to death and blamed the angels for taking her away. Yet still, he goes out to the tombs and sleeps near her grave night after night. And here is Hamlet laid open. His father's ghost has penance to pay for crimes committed during his lifetime. I really don't know our ghost girl's story yet, but somehow this last doesn't seem to fit. And if she was only in her young teens when she died, I can't believe it is a love interest that keeps her haunting our school. Maybe the thread that ties it all together is that someone needs to pay for what happened. A vengeance that needs to be settled. According to what I have heard, this girl's death was an unfortunate accident. There was no evil intent on the janitor's part, but maybe this girl, this ghost girl, doesn't understand that. Maybe she is still trying to get him back somehow for her untimely death. I'm not really sure what to make of any of this, but I know I need to get these books picked up before Mrs. Douglass gets here. I don't want her to begin the day creeped out. I've just gotten started reshelving the books when I hear footsteps. I look up as Mrs. Douglass appears over the tops of the floor shelves.

"Good morning, Mr. Rodriguez. I thought I heard someone back here. The poetry books again, huh? I wander what the deal is with those?" She asked, with a generally pleasant look on her face. Whatever had been going on the last time I saw her was past, I guess. It was like her denying that books were down the last time we talked never happened. At least it didn't register on her face.

"O, good morning, Mrs. Douglass. I was just cleaning these books up off the floor. I didn't want you to have to do it first thing when you got in this morning," I replied, smiling up at her in relief.

"Did you find anything interesting, or was it just a heap of books?" She asked.

"Well now, it was all poetry books like before, but a couple of them were turned open to some rather interesting choices, I thought." She was almost gliding over me now, it seemed, as I worked my way up to a standing position.

"Do tell, Larry. They have all been just thrown down, or so it seemed when I've had to pick them up." She queried.

"Hmm, well, Edgar Alan Poe's book was open to a poem called "Annabelle Lee." We had to memorize it way back when I was in school. And This collection of Shakespeare's work was open to "Hamlet." I thought that was kind of interesting, considering the recent activities here at the middle school. Do you think that was just a coincidence, or could there be something to it?" I asked, shaking my pants legs back down from having been down on my knees.

She pushed her dark hair back and leaned back against the opposite shelf. She sighed. "Mr. Rodriguez, I don't know exactly, but it is scaring me a little. You know, it feels like there's a presence in here sometimes, and I don't like it. Please don't tell anybody I said that. I don't want them to think I'm crazy. I'm already the new kid in town, trying to work through all that "let me be one of you' business, but It just comes over me, and this is going to sound crazy, so don't you tell a soul, or I promise, I'll come back and haunt you!" She said with a nervous laugh. I was laughing almost the same way, especially after how she was looking at me the other day. Like she was possessed or something. Now it was as if she were admitting that she felt it too. "You know, Larry, it's like she is searching for something, and she wants to use me to help her find it," she said.

"Then I guess we know that she is a pretty smart ghost. Using the librarian to help do research sounds pretty clever to me." I said.

"I know, right? I'm not saying I'm the smartest around or anything, but I do have access to lots of information." She paused and stood back up off the shelf she had been leaning on. She pulled out the collection of Poe poems. "Annabelle Lee, you say. The guy in that poem was searching for lost love. First, I guess, but he was also seeking peace. If the story I have heard about this girl is true, then she was a seventh grader that got stuck behind the bleachers when they closed up after a game one night, right?" she asked.

"That's what I've heard. Do we know what year that happened? I thought if we could find that out, we could maybe find her picture in the yearbook and find out about her family, that kind of thing. Maybe it would help us help her find what she is looking for." I said all this like it was printing out of me from a copy machine. It felt very weird, and when I looked up, Mrs. Douglass was looking at me very closely.

"Larry, it looked for a moment there that you weren't really here. Did you feel something weird, or what?" She asked, very concerned.

"Hmm. You know, it was like I was in the room listening to what I said, not like I was the one saying it. You don't think this girl did that to me somehow, do you?" I asked a bit more than just concerned. I didn't like the idea of being a conduit for spiritual activity. It made my spine tingle.

Suddenly she had this memory come back to her, and she said, "O no, Mr. Rodriguez, the other day, I felt like the same thing happened to me. You were in here, and I remember giving you the evil eye. I suddenly remember telling you that there were no books on the floor when you asked. Why did I do that? Until just now, I didn't even know that I did."

"Yeah, I remember; I was big time confused, but I had decided to just put it off on the differences between men and women, and that was why I didn't have a clue why you denied it happened. I even wondered if I had just imagined you telling me that. Several times, I think, you said it happened. But I was trying to blame it on my being too tired. Too overworked or something," I said.

"Well, the thing is, that wasn't me doing that. I mean, I'm sorry, I could tell you were freaked out, and I'm not trying to make excuses, but that wasn't me," she said. She blew a tuft of her hair back from her brow and sighed deeply.

"It's like this girl has some kind of energy that uses us to help her get unblocked from whatever has kept her here all these years. Why this is happening now, or maybe it has been happening to others, and we just don't know about it." I said.

The room seemed to close in on me as I mentioned these things to Mrs. Douglass.

"Hey, I've got to get out of here," I said. She could see that I looked nervous.

"Are you going to be alright?" She asked.

"Sure, everything is fine. I'm fine. I just have to, you know, get to those bathrooms. Can't ever tell what those kids are going to do next in there," I said as a way of escape. I hustled out of the library. It's crazy, but I mean, I could hardly breathe in there all of a sudden. This girl ghost has got a grip on me in a way unlike anything ever in my life. Part of me wants to help her find resolve, and another part of me wants to get away from her and never look back. What exactly is happening? I bent down in the hallway and put my hands on my knees. "God," I said. "Help me get a grip. I can't beat this thing. I am helpless without you against the spiritual forces, but my eyes are on you." I remembered then the prayer of Jehoshaphat. "O LORD, God of our ancestors, are you not God in heaven? Do you not rule over all the kingdoms of the nations? In your hand are power and might so that no one is able to withstand you." He goes on to say that these great hordes have come against

God's people, and then he asked God if he would not execute judgment against them. It picks up again, saying, "For we are powerless against this great multitude that is coming against us. We do not know what to do, but our eyes are on you." Thank you. Lord, for your word." I remember my momma teaching me, "Thy word have I hidden in my heart that I might not sin against you." That scripture came from Psalms 119. I guess that is the longest chapter in the Bible and full of reasons why we need to keep God's Word close to our hearts. I got my breath and went back into the library. Mrs. Douglass had gone back to the checkout desk. She was leaning against this post that was situated exactly in the middle. She looked exhausted. "Mrs. Douglass. Mrs. Douglass, I am sorry for running out like that. To be honest, I was scared. But God has reminded me, once again, that he has got this. Don't be afraid, Mrs. Douglass. He is greater than all this mess and then some."

She looked up at me, surprised to see me back so soon. "It's going to be okay, Mrs. Douglass. I just needed to tell you that before I go on to my other duties," I said. She was still staring at me, and then she smiled.

"Thanks, Mr. Rodriguez. I needed to hear that just now," she said. And with that, I was once again out the door.

Chapter 12

"How did your day go, Lorenzo?" My wife asked when I came home that evening. She's the only one that ever calls me Lorenzo. My mother used to call me that, but my dad and the rest of my family always just called me "Larry." So, it kind of feels special when my wife uses a name for me that only she uses. It kind of makes me feel more at home. She was dressed in jeans and a green flannel shirt, with long sleeves with that square pattern they seem to always have. Her hair was in a ponytail, and she had on her red Ked sneakers. She had been out in the yard raking the mulberry leaves, and the scent of fall was on her. My wife is the reason I come home every night, I realized, and a very good reason it is. Thinking about her just now made me back up a little and decide not to unload all the burdens of my day.

"Ahh," I said with a sigh. "How did my day go? I'll tell you about it later, sweetheart. Just seeing you when I come home makes every day better. How did your day go?" I asked. She smiled, and then her face turned pensive. She remained quiet for a moment. Nudging her a bit, I said, "Well, I know that you've been busy in the yard." I paused and lifted my head. And one thing went very well. Whatever you have in the oven is the aroma of heaven."

She smiled again and said, "Sweetheart, you really are the best part of my life. I love you, you crazy thing." Again, she paused a bit and then said, "Honey, I got word today that my sister is very sick. They don't expect her to make it." She said this was super tough because the one sister that she has left is the one that she has always been closest to. She managed to hold it together until I reached out and touched her. At my touch, she broke into sobs and reached over and clung to me. I took her in my arms and let her cry. She cried for a long time like she was crying out all the memories of her childhood and maybe even the lost time since she was in the States and her sister back home in Mexico.

"O, honey, I'm so sorry. What happened?" I asked, rubbing her back through her soft flannel shirt.

She wiped her eyes on her sleeve. I spied a box of tissue on the kitchen counter that wasn't there when I left this morning. No doubt this wasn't her first cry of the day. I grabbed a couple of them and handed them to her. Taking them from me, she said, "Thank you, Honey, you're always so sweet. Umhmm," she said with a sign, "I don't know all the details, but her husband called and said she just collapsed. He rushed her to the hospital, and the doctor told him that she had had a severe heart attack. Her heart is very weak. Larry, I don't know what to do. I just talked to her last weekend, and she sounded fine. We were planning on going down there for Christmas, you know, but now..." She trailed off, tears splashing down on my pants leg as I held her.

I looked at my wife, and I saw her tears. I knew how she loved her sister. I had lost my closest brother some years ago, and for me, it was like tearing out my heart. I knew her pain would be no less. I had to be here for her during this time. Just then, I was aware of the wind blowing in the mulberry trees outside our house. My spirit seemed to join the gentle sway as I held my wife in my arms. We swayed gently, letting the wind sing to us, soothing our cares and pain. Though it was my wife who was about to lose someone very special to her, as her husband of so many years, I felt one with her, and my heart ached along with hers.

"O Lord God, creator of heaven and earth, he who gives life and takes it away, have mercy on us now. Give us peace, knowing that you are the one who holds us in your hands. Father, we ask that you give assurance to Rosa's sister, Maria, tonight. May she rest in your arms even as I hold the gift of my heart that you gave me o so many years ago. Lord, let her feel your presence all around her now. Before her, behind her, within her. Whether in your infinite wisdom you take her or leave her with us, give her the assurance that you are with her and that she will never be alone. O father, how we love her. How my wife Rosa's heart goes out to her sister right now...." I trailed off. I could feel my wife at ease within my arms, and then she turned to face me and continued the prayer: "Yes, Father, my heart goes out to Maria. As much as I love her, I know that you love her all the more. Thank you for the gift she has been to me all these years. Lord, how I will miss her if she goes now to be with you, but Father, I trust her to you. There is no place we would rather be than with you. We live our days before you here, and we will happily live them before you in the next life. Thank you for your son, who has made this possible. It is in his name that we come before you."

Together we said, "Amen." Just that simple act of prayer, calling out to God in harmony, had given us both a sense of peace.

"I think that you should go to her, Rosa, how she would love to look upon your face now. Yours is the face of an angel. She will either believe that God has sent you to heal her or to help her across the Jordan into Canaan. I will buy a ticket for the bus trip. Chihuahua is not so far away. You could be there tomorrow afternoon. I will follow you there this weekend," I said, caressing her arms and shoulders. Though my income is not much, we have managed our money bit by bit over the years so that when trouble comes like this, we are able to weather the storm.

"Thank you, Lorenzo. O how I love you, my love. You are such a comfort to me. Thank you for praying with me. It has given me such peace that I have not felt for so long. God surely sent you to me," she said.

Reflecting as I continued to hold her, I thought about this crazy ride we call marriage. Rosa and I have been married since we were kids ourselves. We hardly knew any life when we were not together. There have been many times, and for a lot of years, when we've struggled, trying to figure out how to be true to our own selves and still be true to one another. It has been a turbulent dance at times, and many have been a time when we had to just sit the dance out for a bit. How many times did we pray, together, and even more, apart from each other, asking God to help us make some sense of each other and our own selves? We wanted to honor God with our marriage, but o what a struggle that has been! But look at us now! I am so happy that, despite us, somehow, out of the mess that we created, God brought us together, and the bond between us is now cemented together with the Holy Spirit of God. Please don't think I am blowing my own horn. This is all God's doing. I love this woman, and she loves and respects me. I praise God for this gift. I helped Rosa up and walked her to the bedroom. "Honey, why don't you go ahead and get ready for bed. I'll get on the phone and get your ticket," I said.

Rosa responded, "Thanks, Lorenzo. I appreciate it," and with that, she headed into our master bathroom to get ready for bed.

I got on the phone and ordered the ticket for my wife. Bus tickets are usually less expensive than airline tickets, so when the ticket agent said, "That will be two hundred and ninety-eight dollars. The number on your card, please?" I was caught off guard.

I responded, "I'll be paying with my Visa card. "Humm, did you say two hundred and ninety-eight dollars?"

"Yes, sir. Is there a problem?" She asked.

"No. No, I need to purchase the ticket, but that just sounded high for a one-way bus ticket from La Plata to Chihuahua." I waited for a response, but there was none. "Okay," I continued, "here's the number." With that business complete, I got off the phone and went to give Rosa the information. I figured I would not mention the cost. When it came right down to it, we would have bought the ticket no matter what the cost. Rosa did not feel comfortable driving in Mexico, especially in the big cities of Juarez and Chihuahua. The roads are a bit narrower and often not as well maintained. I really can't blame her. When we go down together, my sense of awareness is automatically heightened. Running off a highway with no shoulder and a big drop-off can cause a vehicle to roll or get torn up pretty badly. But those bus drivers are road warriors. They drive with complete confidence and act like the narrow roads don't bother them at all. They amaze me. Rosa will be safe riding with them. The bus would leave at six a.m. While she got ready to go, I packed her a lunch and water bottle to take with her. We got ourselves ready for bed and turned in rather late. It was almost eleven p.m. when we went to bed. We knew that we both needed a good night's sleep but also knew that times like these were often hard times to still the mind and get to sleep. I set the clock for four thirty a.m., and we turned out the light. As we lay there on our backs after turning this way and that, we began to hear the rain fall softly on the house, the wind still blowing gently in the trees. It really was just like the angels of God had surrounded our house to still our troubled hearts. The scripture again came to mind: "Why are you afraid, you of little faith?" Then he got up and rebuked the winds and the sea, and there was dead calm. They were amazed, saying, "What sort of man is this? That even the wind and the sea obey him?"

Before I knew it, the alarm was going off. Both of us sat up and smiled. We knew that God had once again given us the gift of a good night's sleep despite everything. And there was something else. There was peace in our hearts that no matter what, today was in God's hands. I remembered the verse from Psalm 118: "This is the day that the LORD has made, let us rejoice and be glad in it."

While my wife got dressed, I put on the coffee and heated up some cinnamon rolls she had made for us the day before. The aroma of the coffee and cinnamon mixed together gives the house a wonderful homey smell. Rosa came out dressed and ready for her trip. She wore a warm waist-length jacket that was made of cotton and zipped up in the front, keeping out cool air. It was one I had bought for her At the Mescalero Apache Convenience Station before you go on up the mountain to Ruidoso. It bore lines of red and green and yellow and blue. I had stopped at the station to get coffee when traveling up to spend a weekend in one of the cabins up there on our anniversary a couple of years ago. Rosa had gone to sleep, and her steady breathing convinced me that I would soon join her if I didn't get some caffeine in my body, despite the fact that we were no more than twenty miles from our destination. She was surprised and pleased when I presented it to her when we got out of the car. It was cold when we arrived at our cabin, and she had forgotten her jacket on the kitchen table as we were loading up, it turned out. That was one moment of thoughtfulness on my part that sort of accidentally worked out. I slipped that jacket on her as she got out of the car, and we went into our cabin, me with my arms snug around her. It made me feel proud to be her man, and I know that she was pleased with me too. Sometimes, things just seem to work out. Later, when I woke up in the night to go to the bathroom, I lay awake for a while after I returned to bed. I made sure to give credit where it was due. "God, you know that thing you did back there in Mescalero, setting me up in good standing with my wife on our anniversary. I won't forget that," I told him. And as I look at Rosa now, once again snug in that mountain jacket, I remember and thank him again. It is good to live in the presence of the Almighty.

Because we had gotten up ahead of the alarm, we had a few minutes, so we enjoyed the moment together.

"Sweetheart, thanks for getting the cinnamon rolls and coffee together. Don't they smell terrific together?" She asked.

"Marvelous! Thanks for making the buns yesterday. You make the best! How do you feel? Are you ready for this?" I asked.

"Yes, yes, I am. Thanks for being here for me, especially last night. I was a mess, but you helped me remember the One who holds us in his hands. I know it's going to be alright." She said.

"You still look good in that Jacket," I said.

"Thanks," she responded. "My boyfriend bought it for me."

She winked at me, and as if on cue, we headed out to the truck, packing in her bag and snack, and away we drove to the bus station.

We have both taken this trip so many times. When a family has been sick, when there have been deaths, when we have gone down to work building new church buildings by mixing concrete using a shovel and wheelbarrow or pulling wire to get electricity into yet another new room in relatives' homes, or helping in our old neighborhoods in whatever way was needed. Mexico is a poor country in many ways, especially where she grew up outside of Chihuahua in the mountains, but the people care about each other. I'm not saying it's perfect, but my wife and I are proud of where she comes from.

Once we get to the station, I walk up to the booth with my wife and make sure she gets her ticket. It's ten minutes until six when we walk over to the pick-up point. There are several others there who look a bit weary, but all seem amiable. When the bus pulls up and opens its double doors, I give my wife a tight hug.

She looks up at me, and we kiss. "Just keep doing that," she says. "I want to live in your embrace for the rest of my life." Her eyes are teary, but she just smiles.

"I love you, my love," I say. "I'll see you Saturday, Lord-willing. I'll be praying for you and your sister. Via con Dios!"

"Adios, mi Corazon," she says as she mounts the bus steps. I watch her as she walks back into the bus to find her seat.

"Via con Dios, mi esposa!" I call back.

Shaking myself from my trance, I head back to the truck. It is now ten after six. It will take only ten minutes or so to get across town and to the school door. The blessing of living in a smaller town, especially if you can get ahead of the work crowd. When I get there, I see that Mr. McCrank is already there. I expected this. He is as regular as a clockwork. When I go in the front door, he is there to greet me.

"About time you got here, Rodriguez," he says good-naturedly.

"Good morning, sir," I say. I took my wife down to the bus station this morning. Her sister is very sick down in Chihuahua."

His smile drops and is replaced with a look of concern. "Larry, I am so sorry to hear that. Will she be okay? Do you need to go with her? We can make this happen here if you do." His concern for me is very much appreciated. He is a gruff old Navy veteran, but he is a good man, and I am honored to work with him.

"She will be okay, Mr. McCrank. Thank you. I plan to head down there on Saturday morning. I might need to take days off next week, but I will call it in. I don't like to miss work, but death and sickness are never convenient." I said.

"You got that right, old buddy. Well, just let me know. If you are up to it, I'd like to tell you what I found out," he said.

"About what, sir? I asked.

"About the ghost girl, we have here at Patton. You might find it interesting," Mr. McCrank said.

"O, yes, sir. I'm sorry." I still had my mind on Rosa and her sister. yWhat did you find out?" I asked with refocused interest.

Chapter 13

"Larry, I couldn't get this craziness out of my mind. All week this has been bothering me. I didn't want to talk to anyone about it because I didn't want to start a panic or, maybe worse, make people think I was going crazy. I'm really glad you have been here to talk about this. But yesterday, I left earlier than I usually do, around four thirty in the afternoon, and headed over to the Thomas Branigan Library. I just had to know if there was anything on record about this girl's death. I went up in the stacks and talked to the attendant there. She pointed me to microfiche files that had all the local paper news back to its inception in 1881. I figured that would do it." He paused a minute to catch his breath, I think.

"1881. Wow! I wouldn't have guessed that. Well, how did it go? What did you come up with?" I asked.

"Funny, but it sort of circled me around back to the school here," he said.

"How's that?" I asked.

"So, I dug back to when our school started in the fall of 1960. No need to look back beyond that. I worked from that end until I got to 1972. On November 9, 1972, the Sunday edition recorded an accident at Patton Junior High that occurred the previous Friday night. The article said that following a basketball game between

Patton and Sierra Junior High, a young girl was killed after being crushed by the new electric bleacher system that had been installed at Patton the summer before. The Janitor, Lee Goodland, had swept up the gymnasium after everyone left and was moving back the bleachers in order to finish up for the night. He had already moved the visitor's bleachers back and swept up there and was just moving the home side in when he heard a terrible cry. He hurriedly shut the bleachers off. The cry came again, this time barely audible.

"Umm, help me," it said. He rushed over to the bleachers and saw that a young girl was caught between the bleachers and the wall. Blood was pouring out on the gym's wooden floors. The girl looked at him with waning eyes.

"Hold on! Hold on! Just a minute. I'll back it up," his wife told reporters. He hurried back to the controls and reversed the bleachers, opening them wide. Quickly he rushed back to help the girl, but when he got to her, she had expired, according to the news report."

"Wait. You said his wife told the reporter what happened. Why didn't they question the man?" I asked.

"Seems the janitor was very distressed after what happened," Mr. McCrank said.

"Yeah, I guess so. Who wouldn't be?" I said.

"Anyway, He called his wife, asking her to call the ambulance. He was so distraught and didn't know how to get the number. Back then, if you didn't have someone's number, you had to find it in a phone book or call the operator, remember? Seems like forever ago. I guess he couldn't find the phone book and maybe forgot about calling the operator. Remember, this was way before the 911 system was put into place. Anyway, he told his wife all this stuff. She said it just came rushing out of him. She had to shush him so she could get off and call the police. She said later in another interview that she would never have gotten off the phone with him if she had known it would be the last time she ever saw him. he just up and disappeared. No one ever heard from him again," Mr. McCrank concluded.

"No way! He just took off? You have got to be kidding? That sure made this whole thing look suspect!" I bellowed.

"I guess so. Who knows what happened? Maybe a foul play. It's all a mess, but if there is a ghost girl at this school that is stirring so much up all the sudden, it is my guess that somehow this event is connected to it, you know," he said.

"What about his wife, the janitor's, I mean? Did he ever get back in touch with her? Surely, he did. Where is she now?" I asked.

"Well, I, I don't know. That was all that issue of the paper said. As of that last interview, I think it was in April of 1973, and she still hadn't heard from him. I looked forward to a few more weeks in the paper, but I didn't find anything else about the janitor and his wife. The paper did list the name of the janitor as Lee Goodland, and his wife's name was Juanita. The little girl's name was withheld until they were able to notify the next of kin," Mr. McCrank said.

"That just doesn't make any sense. Where was that girl from if her next of kin had to be notified? It seems like her momma would have been up at that school that night wondering where her little girl had gotten off to. No way would her parents just not be available, would they?" I almost shouted back.

"Larry, I don't know the facts; I'm just telling you what I read. It may be that there is more in later editions of the paper; I just didn't want to stay there all night. I did look all the way through 1973 and didn't find anything. It may have been that I was just too tired and missed it somehow. Honesty, I haven't been sleeping too well of late," he said, almost in apology.

"I'm sorry, Mr. McCrank. I am glad you took the time to find something out. If we could find the janitor or his wife, maybe we would have a better clue of what to do about all this. I don't know," I said. I'll see if I can do a find-a-grave search using his name. Maybe it will show the janitor or his wife or something. You said his last name was Goodland, is that right?" I asked.

"Sure, that's right. Lee and Juanita Goodland. That would be great, Larry. In the meantime, I will do a little investigating with some of the old heads around here and a couple of administrators that I know of that have since retired. Maybe they can help me turn up something. Maybe someone remembers the little girl's name. I don't know. At least it will be good to feel like we are doing something to move things forward on this business," he said.

"Sounds good, boss. Thanks for helping me team up on this. I would sure like for things to get back to normal around here; well, as normal as a middle school can get. Talk to you later," I said.

"Later, Larry," Mr. McCrank said. And then he added, "Larry, keep me updated on your wife and her sister. I hope everything works out."

Thanks, Boss. I appreciate it," I said and headed on out to tackle the day that lay ahead.

Chapter 14

"How are you doing, Mrs. Montes?" I asked as I saw her coming down the hall to her room. Her hair was a bit out of place, and her blue blouse had the collar turned in. She must have been in a hurry to get back to work this morning. She seems to always work late and come in early. Her commitment to teaching is commendable. I had been doing a quick dust mopping of the science hall before the kids came in. The winds from last night had stirred up a bit of dust before the rains came. There would be mud on every shoe that came through the door today. I had mats at the doors, but, well, this is just part of the job.

She was rustling in her purse as she came down the hall. She looked up, flustered. "O, I'm fine, I guess, Larry." She blew up a tuft of hair that had fallen down into her face. "I just can't seem to find my room key this morning. I always take it home with me because I lock my door as I leave each evening. You know I tend to stay late, and most of the time, my trash has already been gathered and the floor vacuumed by the time I leave."

"Don't worry about it, Mrs. Montes; I can open your door." I picked out my master key and opened her door. It creaked a little when it swung open. "There you go. Sorry about that creak. I guess I need to get some 3-in-1 oil on that door today," I said.

"Thanks, Larry, you're the best. What would we do here if we didn't have you cleaning up after us and rescuing apparently absent-minded teachers like me?" she said with a smile. She stepped into her room, and I continued on down the hall with my dust mopping, but then I heard Mrs. Montes call out to me again.

"Hey, Larry. Would you come to look at this?" A look of concern crossed her face.

"Yes, ma'am. I'll be right there." I turned and leaned the dust mop against the wall and hustled down to her room. "Is everything okay?" I asked as I entered her room.

"Yes, everything is alright." She said, her voice trailing off a bit. "Would you look here? Right there. My keys were just laying right there on the corner of my desk like I had left them there. I wear my room key on a lanyard and keep my car key in my purse; it's a keyless remote." She paused and looked at me, almost helpless. "The thing I can't figure out is how did I lock my door if I left my room key on my desk? I guess you must have locked it, huh?" She asked.

"Well, I do lock a lot of doors every night, Mrs. Montes. If you didn't lock it, I must have. I am so glad you found them, Mrs. Montes." I said, not remembering having locked her door last night, but I wasn't going to tell this poor flustered lady that.

I paused a minute as I watched her.

She was so lost in her thoughts. "Well, I better get back to work, Mrs. Montes. Have a good rest of your day. I am so glad that your keys are found," I said as I backed out of the room. I heard her continue to talk, mutter really, as I left the room.

"You too," she said. "I just don't understand it. This is so unlike me. I never forget my keys, and I could just swear that I locked that door last night."

I hustled on down the hall, my dust mop leading the way. "I guess this is just another strange start to the day," I thought to myself. I shook my head as if that might set things straight. I shifted my thinking to my wife. "I hope Rosa is alright. I guess she has crossed the border by now. She should be in Chihuahua by what? Around three or maybe even two this afternoon if everything goes just right. You can never tell. There's the border crossing, to begin with. That used to go so smoothly but now, ever since 911, when the terrorists brought down the World Trade Center Buildings in New York, and the Pentagon got hit, and the fiery crash in the fields of Pennsylvania…at least that road down to Chihuahua is very scenic, I think, but they don't have much of a pull off lane, and if you go off the road, at least in some points, well, it's a very harsh drop. Lots of rollovers on the road like that. But I'm sure that bus driver has made the trip so many times he could do it with his eyes closed. That's the bus route the Chihuahua to El Paso and even on up to our town takes every day.

So, I'm sure she will be fine. Nevertheless, she will be on my mind and in my heart, all day, bless her heart. Her sweet sister means so much to her, but we are all getting older. I guess time catches up with us all," I thought as I continued on with my morning duties.

I broke out of my muse as I heard Mr. Jackson coming down the hall, his tennis shoes squeaking a little with every step. "Hey, Larry, good morning! You sure have this place looking great! I sure hope we don't make too much of a mess of the place as we come in today. That rain last night sure muddied things up. But hey, nothing like a little job security, right?" He said with his wry little laugh.

"Yeah, right," I said, a little sarcasm in my voice. "Got to love that job security."

That Mr. Jackson, he's always got a smile for everybody and would help me clean the building if I got in a jam, I really do believe that. He's just that kind of guy. Schools need more smiles and positive attitudes. There's always plenty to worry about and fuss about. Especially if you hang out in those little circles of teachers that always seem to be whispering to themselves. My advice to new teachers is to avoid those like the plague. They will only make you wonder why you picked your profession and have you looking for an out before your first year of teaching is over. I've seen it happen to several young aspiring teachers. They just want to fit in. If only they knew what they were trying to fit into, they might seek alternative routes. It takes seeing things from a different perspective to keep smiling. Somehow or another, Mr. Jackson has figured that out, I guess. I catch up with him as he is about to enter his classroom in the seventh-grade hall.

"Hey, Mr. Jackson, any more T.V.s turning off and on, you know, that kind of weird stuff you and Mr. Rigsby were talking about a few days ago? Any more ghost appearances in your room?" I asked.

"Hmm," he smiled rather nervously. "I, a, no, I don't think so. O, did you hear Mr. Rigsby telling me that the other morning? Yeah, that's right, you were out in the hall sweeping. That was quite a wild tale. You know, I have felt, more than seen, a presence in my room. Now, remember you asked me. You're not going to go spreading this around or anything, are you?" He asked.

"No, no, Mr. Jackson," I said with a nervous laugh. "I just want to know what's going on around here. I've heard about different things. Tell me what you mean by 'feeling a presence.'" "So, my room is called 'The Chapel,' right? You know that. Now I want to make it clear that I am a believer in Jesus Christ, I know you are too, Larry, so I feel comfortable talking to you about these things. And because I believe what the Bible says, I know that each of us has a spirit living within us; it is who we are, really. And I know that when we die, our spirit returns to the one who gave it. God.

God gives us life, and he takes it away. I'm comfortable with that. I like knowing that God has me in his hands, and I am not just here, somehow, and one day will die, and that will be it. But anyway, my room is sometimes just filled up with the presence of God. I know he is here. My kids sense it too. This is a spiritual place, Mr. Rodriguez. That sounds crazy in a public school, right? But it is so, just the same. With that in mind, recently, I have felt another spirit here. It is not a spirit that I fear. Now I know what Mr. Rigsby said the other morning sounded creepy, but I think the spirit was just messing around. It's a girl. I've talked to her several times when I've felt her presence. So far, it's a one-way conversation, but I talk to her just the same. I don't summon her or anything. It's just when I feel her presence and I'm alone, I talk to her. I don't want anyone thinking I'm crazy. But since you asked, she has been coming more and more in the last couple of weeks. I don't know if this is a special time for her, you know, like with the Day of the Dead stuff that is coming up, but she is definitely here, and you know what else, Larry? I think she wants help. I believe that somehow, I might be able to help her. I think she feels it too, so she comes back, again and again. So, am I crazy, or what?" He asked. When he looked up at me, his face was glowing, like the presence of God was on him at that very moment.

I sure hadn't expected all that I got from Mr. Jackson, but I knew after just listening to him for just a little while that I had come to the right place. Maybe it was God's prompting that had me call after him.

"Mr. Jackson, you are not crazy. If anything, you seem to be one who has eyes to see and ears to hear, as Jesus talks about. That girl is real, Mr. Jackson. Too many other things have happened to demonstrate that. As you said, I don't believe she is evil either, but sometimes I do believe she gets bored and messes with some of the teachers a bit. I also think she is looking for something, and you have to be right that she is trying to find her peace. For some reason, she seems to have gotten trapped here, closed in, and unable to return to the God who gave her life. Mr. Jackson, do you remember the passage in Hebrews that says all angels are spirits in God's service, sent to serve those who inherit salvation? It's at the end of chapter one," I said.

"Yes, I remember that passage, Larry. What do you think about it?" He asked.

"Well, sir, I think that God has put you here at this time to serve the kids of our town and neighborhood and that this little girl who has been trapped here somehow is just someone else that God wants you to help get to where she needs to be. I believe that you, sir, are God's angel sent to help this girl get home to her Father," I said, my eyes shining and my spirit agreeing as my spine tingled at the words that had just come out of my mouth.

He looked at me and said, "Larry, you said I was one who had eyes to see and ears to hear. I believe that, too. I don't mean to brag by saying that. It's just that I am at this point in my life, in the flow of what God is doing more than at any point in my life. I feel God's pleasure. I think you know that feeling, Larry. God works in and through you here at this school. He has for years. You give teachers and administrators a quiet calm that we all need so much. Larry, what if you and I decide right here and right now that we are going to work together to help this girl make it home? Could you get together with me to pray this girl home? I don't know what the problem is, but I know that God is bigger than whatever it is. I also know that where two or three come together in his name, there he is in their midst."

"Amen. God is here, right now," I said, "Approving what you just said. I feel his presence." "As do I." He replied.

"Mr. Jackson, I can meet you after school one day this week. I can stay late because my wife is out of town. Since you are a praying man, would you please pray for my wife and her sister? Her sister's health took a sudden unexplainable turn for the worse. I don't know what happened exactly. Her husband said the doctors told him that she had had a heart attack, and they didn't expect her to make it. I put my wife on a bus to Chihuahua this morning. I will join her this weekend, Lord-willing, and may miss a few days next week. I've already talked to Mr. McCrank about it," I said.

His eyes shone with tears as he looked at me like he could see into my soul. "Sure, Mr. Rodriguez, let's pray right now. He closed his eyes and put his hand on my shoulder, and prayed: Merciful God, how happy we are that you are here with us right now. Father, please make Larry's wife aware of your presence with her right now as she rides that bus down to Chihuahua. Father, settle your peace down on her. May your light shine through her as she looks upon her sister, and Lord, may I be so bold as to ask you to raise her sister up. Marvel the doctors and family that are gathered around and bring glory to your name. Father, in Jesus' name, we ask you to drive out the sickness in her body and fill her with the healing that only comes through you, our Great Physician. Father, I praise you that you have given us the privilege to come boldly to your throne and ask in Jesus' name. Amen."

I felt the charge of God's Spirit in that room right then. "My God, I know that you are always with me, but how awesome it is to feel your presence," I said.

Mr. Jackson smiled at me and said, "Amen to that, brother." He gave my shoulder a squeeze and said, "Have a good day, brother. God is in your corner."

I left his room then and headed back to my closet. I thought about the books that were likely on the floor in the library. If I hadn't spent so much time talking to first, Mr. McCrank, and then

Ms. Montes, and just now, with Mr. Jackson, I would have gone to clean them up, but as it was, the time had flown up to eight a.m. and several other teachers had already arrived. In fact, I figured Mrs. Douglass must already be in there, getting ready for her first classes. She had probably already picked them up. I'd ask her about the poetry books later.

In my closet, I took out some cleaning supplies and got my mop heads ready. After last night's rains, the mud would be tracked in, and I needed to be ready to keep it cleaned up to prevent tracking all up and down my halls. I guess I knew it was a futile effort, but I had to try. It is my job to keep this school looking good, showing visitors that, no matter how old our school is and no matter what others think of our old 'ghetto school,' we take pride in it and call it home.

Popping in the lounge right quick, I made sure there was plenty of coffee left for the teachers who straggled in. My wife calls them "Bus dust." Last to arrive, first to leave. Right behind the buses both ways. We really don't have too many teachers like that, mostly the younger ones who haven't learned yet the value of being prepared and comfortable with the day, even before it starts. Some don't want to commit the extra time, but they don't realize what they receive back in peace of mind dividends.

I am at the front door as the bell rings, and the kids are allowed in. Many of the kids will be coming from the cafeteria, which is across the courtyard, to the north of the main building. The cafeteria was built separately, along with the gymnasium, in a climate as mild as ours, where we seldom have single-digit temperatures and where we have only eight inches of rain annually; it's not a big deal to have the structures separate like that.

The kids come in all ready for the day. They have enough energy to power a nuclear plant, I think. Most of them are smiling and laughing. Invariably we have a few wanting to run in, a friend chasing them. "Hey, you kids, slow down now," I say. "Okay, Mr. Larry," they respond, slowing a little and smiling. It seems to be mostly the sixth graders that still need to kind of learn the ropes of how middle school operates. Ms. David is out in the entryway, like she usually is, high-fiving kids and mentioning their new haircuts or shirts. She always does her best to make the kids feel good when they come to school and, in doing so, wins their hearts. They are loyal to Ms. David. She can be hard on them at times, but they know she loves them, and that makes all the difference. And I think love is the right word to use here. She is not married, never has been to my knowledge. Her singular devotion seems to be to this school. She does have a dad who is still living, and she sees him. He also has always been devoted to the schools. I guess maybe he is her inspiration. Funny, I never really thought about that.

When the kids have all made it to their classrooms, a student comes over the intercom system and asks all the students to stand for the pledge. All stand and face the flag. "I pledge allegiance to the flag of the United States of America and to the republic for which it stands, one nation under God, indivisible, with liberty and justice for all." The pledge takes me back to when I was in school, and I never tire of hearing it. There are plenty of things that could be better in our country, but it is true that we are a blessed nation. I think it would be a grand thing if we took more time to recognize how much we have in this country and stopped focusing so much on our perceived shortcomings. Anyway, that's my two cents worth on the matter. After the pledge, a moment of silence is announced, and the kids continue to stand quietly to reflect or pray or just wait, I guess. The announcer then tells them they may be seated, and the announcements come on. Sometimes the principal, sometimes a vice-principal, or teacher will make the announcements. "Don't forget your fundraisers are due in by this Friday"; "The basketball team had a good outing last night. The boys lost a heartbreaker to Sierra 34-35 on a last-minute shot, but they played their hearts out. Great job, guys! The girls won their game 29-18 against the girls of Sierra. That's three wins in a row for our girls! Great job, Cougars!" Stuff like that. Then I hear Mrs. Douglass's voice come over the intercom. "Good morning, students. This is Mrs. Douglass. The library will be closed today. If you have books that are due, student helpers will be coming around to collect those during homeroom. Teachers, I apologize for the late notice. Hopefully, we will be up and running again tomorrow. Thank you." The intercom was silent then, and the silence seemed to echo down the halls. What was this all about? I wondered. Just then, I saw Mrs. Douglass coming out of the front office, making her way through the inner courtyard toward the library. I opened the door to the courtyard and called after her.

"Is everything all right, Mrs. Douglass? Are you okay?" I asked.

She looked back at me, startled. "O, Mr. Rodriguez, I don't know what happened. Can you come to the library and see it? Maybe you know what we should do?" She said. She looked very flustered.

"Okay, right behind you," I said as I hurried to catch up with her. "What's going on?" I asked.

"Just you wait and see," she said. I followed her into the library and back behind the front counter. There, written on the message board, a note had been pinned, written in bright red marker. "Please help me. I've got to find him. I've got to tell him it's not his fault. I've got to tell him I'm okay. I've got to tell him it's okay to live again." It was written in sort of a childish cursive and signed, I think, at the bottom, but the signature, if that's what it was, was illegible.

Mrs. Douglass' face was white as a ghost. "You see, Larry. I haven't even told admin about this crazy thing with the books, and now this. If this library is haunted, I can't let the kids come in like it's no big deal, can I? I just don't know what to do."

"I see what you mean," I said. "So, the admin was okay with you closing the library today?"

"Yes, well, I told them that my system was down and, since we've gone to this new computerized checking out of books, I couldn't account for books going out. They told me to go ahead and gather the books that were due; why I am not sure, really, because if the system is down, how would I check them in? I think they know something is up, but either they are giving me some space to work it out or are too busy to deal with it right now," she said.

"Mr. McCrank knows about this and a whole lot of other stuff that is going on in the building," I said.

"He does?" She asked. She looked at me like I had violated a secret held between us.

"Mrs. Douglass, what is going on in here is only a small part of the crazy things that are going on. Nothing threatening, but lots of upheavals these days as we approach Dia de Los Muertos. I don't know if that has anything to do with it or not, but Mr. McCrank was the first to tell me of something weird that went on in Mrs. Montes' classroom, and since then, he and I have been trying to get to the bottom of this. In fact, He has a lead that we are both going to work on some today," I responded.

"What kind of lead?" She asked.

"Okay. You have the day to figure this out, right? Since the library is closed, could you do some checking? See, we really need to find out about the janitor that was behind the girl's death. Accounts of the event say it was totally accidental, but the man disappeared, and even his wife didn't know what became of him. Some people say he must have gone mad with grief over what happened, and some have said that the man must have murdered the girl, so he fled to keep from being arrested, though no motive was ever given," I said.

"Wow! I knew a little about this, but it seems like the plot is thickening." She paused a minute, looking out into her library as if she might spot the answer there. "Sure, I will do whatever I can to help this poor ghost girl find peace and bring things back to normal here. I called my husband this morning when I found the note. I know it is crazy, but I was crying, hysterical, really. I mean, it's not every day that a ghost writes you a note. I know it's not a threatening note, and this girl doesn't mean me any harm. I know she is just looking for help, but…" she trailed off as she gasped for air. She was crying again. "Larry, I don't even believe in ghosts or didn't. I just don't know how to process any of this."

"Here now, it's okay," I said soothingly. "Hey, I don't think you're crazy. This whole business has me worked up too, but I know that God is bigger than this situation, and I believe that we are being let in on this in order to help this poor girl make her peace and find her family at last. Just this morning, I was talking to Mr. Jackson about all this. He and I prayed about bringing this girl peace. It was a pretty amazing experience. It made me feel like this was all in God's hands, and though we don't know how this is all going to work out, He is going to work it out for his good and somehow use certain ones here at this school to do it." She had stopped crying and was looking at me with wonder in her eyes. "You know, in the Day of the Dead holiday, many believe that there is a window for the dead to come and go between the next life and this one. I think maybe this girl sees this as her opening to the afterlife that she was meant to have. Something stops her, but she is so ready to go home. When Hebrews reads about 'the great cloud of witnesses,' I think that they are there not just to observe but also to assist us in our daily walk. If we can get this girl to her people, she can rest in peace at last." The more I talked, the more Mrs. Douglass relaxed.

I continued. "Hey, Mrs. Douglass, forget about all that research. I can do it after work today. My wife has gone to be with her sister, who is very sick. Please keep her in your prayers. She is really close to this sister. Her name is Maria. But you should go home. Call your husband and go be with him. If you two take time to be together and talk and comfort one another, I believe you will be much better, and maybe, tomorrow when you come back, Mr. McCrank and I will have something and be on the road to resolving this issue," I said.

She looked up at me and said, "Thanks, Mr. Rodriguez. I will go up to the office and see if they will clear my going home. Jim is off today. It will be good to just walk and talk with him about all this," she said. She grabbed her purse and jacket and turned to go up to the office. "Mr. Rodriguez, be careful. And thanks for working to find some resolution to this problem. You know, in a way, it's cool to think we are working to solve a mystery, but I think I'd rather read about solving a mystery than actually be in the middle of it."

I watched her as she headed back through the courtyard back to the main office. Her eyes were still red from crying, and I guess she was doing her best to avoid unnecessary contact with questioning staff members and students. The rumor mill is a very efficient machine. As for me, I had to get back to it and take care of my school business of cleaning and refilling supplies, and then I had my work cut out for me tonight. Something had to come to a head on this, and soon, or we might be looking for a new librarian, I thought.

Chapter 15

At lunch, I gave my wife a call. The service in Mexico is sketchy in places, at best, so I didn't have high hopes that she would be able to receive the call. To my surprise, she answered on the second ring.

"Hello, Larry?" She said.

"How are you, sweetheart? Is the trip going okay?" I asked.

"Yes, everything is going okay, so far, for the most part. It took us a while to get past the border crossing; then, after we got started, there was an accident on the road about a hundred miles south of Juarez. An SUV had rolled. It was pretty torn up. They had a wrecker out there wrenching it up on its bed. I guess it was the guy that had been driving. He was standing nearby, watching it all happen.

He looked a little ruffled up but otherwise alright. He was driving a Subaru Outback, I think. Larry, I have seen commercials about how safe they are supposed to be. I guess maybe they are. It sure worked out for that guy, at least. Since then, we have been rolling right along. The driver came over the intercom a few minutes ago and said we were just over one hundred miles out. I guess we should be there by two this afternoon if all else goes well.

How is your day going?" She asked.

"Well, there's still more to the ghost girl saga, and I'll tell you all about it this evening after I get off from work if you have time to talk. I know this; I'll be glad to have you back. I'm missing you already, but for now, comfort your sister, and may God bless your time with her. I plan on heading your way Saturday morning on the first bus your way," I said.

"It will be so good to have you here with me, Lorenzo. Thanks for understanding about my needing to come down right away," She said.

"You bet, honey, I'll…" just then, we lost the connection. I thought about trying to call back, but I figured we had said what we needed to, and the chances of my getting her again were slim to none. Nevertheless, it was a mercy that I got through at all.

I had made my call from out in the courtyard at one of those blue picnic tables we had set up out there. The temperature was mild today, and I needed a place to talk away from the teachers that were in the lounge. When I got off the phone, I snarfed down my lunch right quick, eager to get back to my work, so I could finish early today and work on that find a grave project I had told Mrs. Douglass about. I had some of Rosa's chicken enchiladas in the fridge, so I tossed them in the microwave and heated them up. There was enough for two left, and I only took one serving, to begin with, but they were so good that I raked the rest of them into my plate, heated them up, and gobbled them down. My Rosa, she makes the best enchiladas. Snarfing has never been so good.

I saw Mr. McCrank while I was out front, sweeping water and fallen leaves away from the entrance. That rain had knocked down a lot of mulberry leaves from our outside lunch area, and the park nearby and seemingly blew the lion's portion of them up into our entrance to the building. And along with all those wet leaves was the remnant of the rain that had fallen last night. I thought if I could clean that mess away, it would save me in the long run, as far as cleaning up inside the building. The wet leaves had a pleasant fall smell, and I would have basked in their aroma if I wasn't on a mission and if I hadn't seen Mr. McCrank speeding off in his Dodge D250 pickup. He had this old 92 Dodge pickup that he was always working on, trying to make it better. "It has great power and the fuel economy; well, Larry, I get twenty miles per gallon," he said to me one day.

"Okay, okay, Mr. McCrank, whatever you say. A man loves his truck. I can't blame him for stretching it out a little bit," I said.

But he wouldn't let it go at that. "No, I'm serious. Of course, I don't drive like a teenager anymore, racing up and down the road to impress my buddies, but when I drive reasonably around town and back and forth to White Oak to visit my wife's people, we get right at twenty miles per gallon. And that old engine (in my opinion, it is the best Dodge ever built) goes up that mountain (he was looking at the Organs Mountains like he was looking up to heaven), Larry it goes up that mountain, even pulling a trailer, and it doesn't miss a beat. Let me tell you something, Larry; you'd do well to shop around and see if you couldn't get you one of these and get rid of that old Ford of yours." Anyway, that's the talk that goes on and on sometimes between fellow truck owners. Whatever. Anyway, I don't know what fire got under his tail to have him heading out of here like that in the middle of the day, but I reckon he has his reasons. I'll ask him about it tomorrow, and maybe he'll have found out some more about our ghost girl.

When I got everything swept up to my satisfaction, I went back inside; the cool wind had gotten under my jacket a bit and made me appreciate the warmth of the school. Ms. David saw me on the fly, off to observe a classroom or have a meeting with a team of teachers or any of the other myriad of assignments she gives herself. She is the driver behind the emotional warmth in this building and has been for years. It's amazing to me that just that quick greeting and smile as she sped down the hall encouraged me and gave me a different kind of warmth about this place. I guess if I was a ghost and somehow got trapped in a place, for whatever reason, this would be the place I would want to be. Maybe that is why our ghost girl has hung out so long. I don't know, but I do know, somehow, I know deep within myself that she wants to be free of this place and this planet and go to her place of rest. How do I know this? Is some kind of spiritual thing going on here?

Without a doubt. I pray that God will help us get her over the Jordan River at last.

I stepped into the front office. "I just saw Mr. McCrank heading out. Is everything okay?" I asked of no one in particular because Miss Riana was running off something on the printer, and Mr. Jackson was in the office, talking to Mrs. Baez about a student in his classroom; it looked to me. Nobody said anything at first, and I realized that I had just blurted out my question without giving any real consideration to what was happening inside. I noticed that there were flowers on the front desk counter with a note reading 'happy twelfth birthday, Britney' on it. Some of these kids are so blessed, I guess. It kind of makes some of the other kids envious, who would never get special notice from their parents no matter what they accomplished. Sometimes I don't know what to think about things like that. Should all have nothing so that all are equal, or would it be better if somehow, we made it so that all had the same to bring about equity. I guess my experience says we can never make things equal, and maybe we shouldn't. We are all on different courses in our lives. We are not the same, nor should we be. The difficulties of life can and should make us stronger, not defeat us. Getting to that place mentally is the challenging part, and, well, I know that is little consolation when times are tough. Like I said, I don't know what to think about things like that. It's one thing to theorize; it is quite another to live out.

Just then, Miss Riana looked up at me and smiled apologetically. "Sorry, Larry. I was trying to make sure all these printed out right. This machine can be temperamental. Now about Mr. McCrank, he has a bad toothache. It's been bothering him for a few days now, but something really set it off today. He called his dentist and was able to get in right away. There had been a cancellation, and it just worked out perfectly for him. He wondered if he wouldn't have to get this one pulled. He said they had been after him the last couple of visits to get a new crown on it, but it was so expensive. It was going to cost him nearly a thousand dollars out of pocket, he said, and that was with insurance. Our dental insurance here leaves something to be desired.

Anyway, I told him he ought to go over to Palomas and get the work done. You can also go over to Juarez; it's just a bigger city and a bit more complicated, so I just stick with Palomas. Anyway, my sister got a crown put on in Palomas for just over three hundred dollars, and that was with no insurance at all. You know, Larry, I'm sure you do. Most of your family still lives in Mexico. Isn't that right?" She asked.

"Yes, ma'am. In fact, most of them live in or very near Palomas. I go there for any dental work I need. My wife does too."

"Is that right? Well then, you know that most of those doctors were trained here in the United States. They do a pretty good job, my sister says. Anyway, that's where he was going in such a hurry. He was in pain." She must have been having a good day, the way she prattled on. She is really one of our caped crusaders around here. If it were not for her heroics, we would crash and burn some days.

"Thanks, Miss Riana. You're the best. You always know exactly what's going on and keep the rest of us straight. As for Mr. McCrank, bless his heart. I had to get a tooth like that pulled a couple of years ago. It was giving me fits, but I went down to Palomas, and they pulled it for me for like fifty-seven dollars, I think. I have been down to Juarez for that kind of work, but the city is so big now, so I went to sleepy little Palomas. I took my wife with me. It gave her a chance to do a little shopping while we were there. I really like that place, and it's much easier to make the border crossing there. Then, of course, while there, we always visit our family." I replied.

"Hey, Mr. Rodriquez, I'm glad you stopped by. I was just going to call you on the radio. Mrs. Ballard in the sixth-grade hall had a kid get sick in her room. She said it was a real mess. Can you go down there with a mop bucket and clean it up? She took her kids out to the lunch area outside tables to finish her class. Her next group will be coming in about fifteen minutes," she said.

"O yeah, yeah, sure, Miss. Riana. I'll head right down there. Gotta love this job sometimes," I said, heading out the door.

"I hate it for you," she called as I was heading out the door. She added, "You're our hero, Larry!" Real loud. Nice to be appreciated. But still. Why do these sixth graders puck so much?

Chapter 16

At the end of the school day, I put out the cones for the buses to come in and direct the parents. Every day it is the same thing. I like seeing the parents driving by, some of whom I've known since they were kids, and also the kids I see every day in the halls as they board their buses, go home with parents or walk to their nearby apartments or houses. Most of the kids at this school come from a lower socio-economical background, but even so, almost all of them are growing up with more than what we had when we were kids. Or it seems that way to me. Why do I say that?

Well, many, if not most of them, have cell phones these days. They are always extracting them from their backpacks or pockets as soon as the bell rings (if not before). And as I check out their clothes, many of them are dressing way better than I did. Some are not, however. I see the kids with shoes that are falling apart or who are wearing clothes way too big or way too small for them. It is pretty clear when it's an attempt at a fashion statement. And it's pretty clear when the kid is just wearing what there is at home to wear.

The bigger shame is that today there are thrift stores everywhere. I can go into a thrift store and, with a little luck, I can come out with some pretty good-looking clothes for less than twenty dollars. Shirt, pants, shoes, even a belt or jacket. And these are within walking distance of their homes. It is some of these same kids that, when asked how their weekend went, tell of having to watch their siblings while their parents and friends drank the weekend away. These same kids have never been over the mountain to Alamogordo, or down to El Paso, or even up to Hatch or T or C. My heart aches for them, and I pray that one day they will break this crazy cycle and do better for their own children. Some will, I guess, but most won't, I figure unless something or someone breaks in on their worlds.

The problem is so big it is intimidating. But maybe it's like the starfish story. A man is walking along the seaside, throwing starfish back into the ocean. Another sees him doing it and says, "You know, you are just wasting your time. You can't throw them all back in. There will be just as many on the shore tomorrow morning. What difference does what you're doing make?" The man who is just casting another starfish into the sea says, "It makes a difference to this one." That's what my wife, Rosa, and I are trying to do. We have this family, the Martinez's, that we live close to. We have invited them over for Thanksgiving dinner, and every few weeks, we invite them over for supper.

It gives us a chance to sort of mentor their parents and find out what they need. We buy shoes for the kids, and I help the dad, Ralph (Raphael), out when he needs work done around his house. He has started doing the same for me. "Many hands make light work," someone said. It's true. Not so much because we always need another set of hands, but because we need the comradery of others.

Wow. I get going on these mind trips. It's a wonder I don't get run over out here directing traffic. No worries. I'm back now. I need to get these cones picked up and head on over to the city library and do some research on our Mr. Lee Goodland, the long-ago former janitor of Patton Junior High. But first, I will call Rosa and see how her trip went and how her sister is doing. Rosa loves her sister, and I am sure she has been wearing God's ear out, praying, and petitioning God for her sister's health and life.

What a woman I have married. She has a heart as big as Texas (no offense, New Mexico) and is always putting others ahead of herself. Why God blessed me so with her, I do not know, but it does help me understand the meaning of grace just a little bit more. "Unmerited favor," the preacher said. "You just don't deserve it, and there is nothing you can do to earn it," he said. That sounds about right. That's my Rosa.

It seemed like the floors were going to take me a very long time to get clean. The rain from the night before and hundreds of students and staff bringing in dirt and mud and sand and leaves…it's a lot. I set my mind to it and worked diligently to get it all cleaned up. When I first started, I almost broke and called Rosa right then, but I really needed to have this finished so I could focus on Rosa. My Rosa. I hated the thought of going home tonight and her not being there.

It took a while. Actually, the day was a little longer than the average one because I had so much to get cleaned up. I just kept telling myself, 'stay with it. Just a few more things to do,' and I counted them off one by one. "Rome wasn't built in a day," I've often heard said.

When I finally finished, I headed out to the truck and fired it up. I gave it a few minutes to warm up as the temperatures had begun to drop with the setting of the sun. It was now quite cool, and I was more than a little hungry. Normally I'd head home, and Rosa would have me a nice supper prepared, but with her down in Chihuahua and my needing to get to the library to do research, I headed over to Lottaburger and got their number one. It comes with fries and a drink and costs less than most chain restaurants. I love their Lottaburger because it is so big and it has lots of onions on it. Delicious. I had a beautiful Coca-Cola to wash it all down. Why does anyone drink those other fountain drinks when Coke is clearly the best? Anyway, I also love that they have that crushed ice. It makes the drink super cold and is good to munch on long after you've finished your meal. I left there and drove on over to the Branigan Library. I made my call to Rosa out in the truck, leaving it running since it had gotten so cool. The library frowns on patrons using their phones inside the library for obvious reasons. It's hard to do research and or read if someone is gabbing to his wife or sweetheart. I get that.

"Honey, Rosa, how has your day gone? Did you make the trip alright? How's your sister?" The questions came out like a flood as I found that I was more eager to hear her voice than I even realized.

"Hello, Larry. It is so good to hear your voice again, too. What has it been now? Five hours?" she teased.

"Oh well, I'm not ashamed to say I miss you and have had you on my mind all day. How are things?" I asked again.

"Honey, Maria is very sick. She is so weak. I've held her hand most of the day and sang songs to her, mixed with prayer. She was just looking at me with almost glazed eyes when I first came, but now, she has talked to me a couple of times and even smiled. She thanked me for singing to her and praying for her. She said she knew I would come. Larry, I am so glad I did. Thank you for sending me on down. I miss you too, honey, but how she needed me! I can feel God's presence in this place as he showers love down on her. I knew I loved her with my whole heart, but I guess I didn't even realize how much that was until I came. I am weak with my love for her. She is my sister. My only remaining sister. Larry, I just can't bear the thought of losing her," she said, choking back her last word.

"Baby, there now. It's okay. God is there with you. He has surrounded you and your sister with his presence. As you were singing over your sister, He was singing over the two of you. He knows your heart, and O, how He loves you. He loves you as much as I love you, Rosa, and many times more! Sweetheart, you are God's child. He will not abandon you," I said. The encouragement I was giving her now seemed to flow out of me as if these were not coming so much from me but straight from heaven.

"I know, Honey, you're right, but I'm just hurting for my sister, and, I guess if I wanted to be honest, I'm hurting even more for myself. How sad it would be not to have her call and hear her sweet voice. A voice that has been there for me in so many ways over the years," she responded.

"You're right, baby; she has been there for you and for us for as long as I have known you and way before that. Maybe even, especially when you and I were not getting along very well. She was the one you called for advice and a listening ear. I even called her myself a few times to get her advice on anniversary and Christmas gifts. I figured she knew you better than anyone.

"So that's how you got so smart about what I liked all these years. You are a rascal! Actually, that was pretty smart. I guess I owe my sister for those times, too," she said pensively.

"Listen, Honey, I just want to share one Bible verse with you, and then I'll let you go. I read this today, and it really spoke to me.

I think it really applies to our situations, yours with your sister and mine, with the craziness at school," I said.

"O Larry, I forgot to ask you about school. Are you still having trouble with that ghost girl?" She asked.

"Yes, well, we are working on figuring it out. I really want to help her find her peace. Mr. McCrank gave me something to work on in that direction, and he is also doing some digging. Mrs. Douglass is also trying to help since her poetry books keep getting knocked on the floor, and Mrs. Montes has had a couple of weird things in her room, and then there's Mr. Jackson, who seems to be handling all this best of all, trusting God to finally give this girl peace. He's got me believing that we really will help her settle things. And I guess that is what led me to this verse I want to share with you," I said.

"Okay, I'm ready," she said.

"Okay, here it is. It is from the New Living Translation. Psalm 34:19 says, 'The righteous person faces many troubles, but the LORD comes to the rescue each time,'" I read.

"The righteous person faces many troubles, but the LORD comes to the rescue each time," she repeated. O Larry, I really like that. I'm going to write that down and put it on the bathroom mirror, and I'll share it with my sister. Thank you, Larry. It seems like the Lord still is speaking loud and clear. I love you, Larry."

"I love you too, Honey. I'll call you again tomorrow. Goodbye, Sweetheart," I said. And hung up the phone. There was a certain peace that came over me then. I felt like somehow; all this was going to work out. "Thank you, God, for the gentle assurances that you give me, day by day," I said.

O, I have to tell you this, at the library, as usual, I had a hard time finding a parking place. This town has a wonderful library, and there have been many improvements to it in the past few years. It is also great that the townspeople utilize this great resource. For me, it's a bit like going back to school every time I visit. It gives me a satisfying feeling. Anyway, I drove around the parking area a couple of times until I saw a lady and her three blond-headed girls coming out of the library with a bag full of books and videos. I waited as I watched them head over to a blue GMC Suburban where they loaded up their goods. I watched as they all seemed in a jovial mood. When I finally got parked, I made my phone call to Rosa, as I said, and then I headed into the library. I saw a couple of other people coming out, books in hand. There was a computer class advertised on Tuesday nights for senior adults and also a reading time for kids in the children's area every Monday and Thursday morning at ten. As I said, this library seemed to always be busy. Back over to the left, just past the main desk, I saw a couple of tutors working with young school-age kids. I headed on back to the back of the library, to the right, where there were books about the history of La Plata and Dona Ana County. I thought I would check back there first. They also had the La Plata Zia News on Microfiche, and I figured I would check that out when I finished with the stacks.

In the stacks, I found a carrel that was unoccupied. I always prefer working in them because they have these little side walls to block distractions which is something I really need most of the time. To find what I needed, I knew I needed to be as specific as possible. I looked for books about Patton Junior High and found one that actually dealt with all the school's founding in La Plata from the inception of the town through the 1980s. I used the index to help me find Patton Junior High, founded in 1960, and saw that jjit really only talked about General George Patton, the man after whom the school was named (if you are not familiar with General Patton, look him up. He is fascinating.) and the capacity of the school, its first principal, stuff like that. It Then went on to give the names of the first teachers at the school, and even the office and cafeteria staff, and finally, at last, as if an afterthought, the janitorial staff. The principal, the teachers, office and cafeteria staff, and even the janitorial staff were all pictured with their names down below. There were only two that worked on the janitorial staff back then. Hector Flores was designated the day janitor, and Lee Goodland served as the evening janitor. There he was. The man who, inadvertently, seemed to start all this ghost girl business at our school. He had dark hair (well, all the pictures were in grayscale, so whether it was black or red or what, I could not be sure) and light-colored eyes. His face was thin, with a bit of stubble on his cheeks, like he hadn't realized he was going to be photographed that day. He wore a dark shirt with button-down pockets with his name, Lee Goodland, printed over the top. Looking into his eyes, I saw a man who had known work and hard times. He had a look of resignation on his face. There was part of me that could relate to him. I wonder what happened to him after that terrible night. I know, except for the grace of God, that the same thing could have happened to any of us who perform the same role. Thank God for his mercy. I sure hope Mr. Goodland found his peace in all this.

There didn't seem to be anything else in the book that would be useful, so I took out my phone and snapped a shot of the page, and put the book away. I headed upstairs, where the microfiche was located. After a little searching, I found the La Plata Zia News and then pulled out the film that had 1970 January to 1972 December. I placed the copy in the machine and began scrolling through. It was page after page of interesting material. I was amazed at how many of the buildings and businesses that were new then had become old and dilapidated or, as was the case of most, had ceased to exist. I found the announcement of Patton Junior High had opened its doors. There were the same pictures here that I had found in the book. Leaving that section, I kept scrolling until I found something on the front page of the Sunday edition. In bold lettering, the headline read, 'Girl Dead at Patton

Junior High. School Janitor Missing.' This was it! I quickly sped down the article. The girl's name was withheld until her parents were notified. So far, attempts to contact them have been unsuccessful. I read on until I got to the part where the reporter was interviewing the Janitor's wife. She was pictured looking flushed and worried. Her husband had called her after the accident. He was very distressed and seemed disoriented. He told about closing up the new bleachers and then hearing the cry. He opened the bleachers back up and found the girl severely injured. He could not save her and kept saying he didn't mean to and that it was all his fault. He asked her to contact the ambulance, and that was the last time she had heard from him. She had no idea where he was, though she had called his parents and brother trying to find him. She did not think her husband to be of a suicidal nature, but he was so distressed. She didn't know what he might do or where he might go. "Whatever happened," She said, "It was an accident, pure and simple."

No leads on his whereabouts after the accident. Searching on through the next year, there was no more mention of the man. Even Googling his name only brought up this same article. There was nothing in the find-a-grave search I did for his name, using approximate dates based on my best guess of his age. It was frustrating, but I made a note to see if maybe someone at school knew of this man's family. Maybe they could help us find out what had happened to him. The good news is that I did finally find the girl's identity. Rosa Maria Rodriguez. There was a picture of a young girl, a bit out of focus, the only one available, from the school annual that year. Again, everything was in grayscale, so it was hard to tell the colors. All I knew for sure was that she had dark hair but, surprisingly, lighter-colored eyes, or so it seemed on grayscale. She was a little thing, no bigger than a mite. She smiled at the camera in a Mona Lisa-type smile, not showing her teeth. She seemed shy but sweet. Someone's sweet little girl. The name certainly gave me the creeps; I can tell you that. She was a Rodriguez, not exactly an uncommon name, but it was my last name, and she held both the names of my wife and her sister. How crazy is that? Again, their names are very common among children of Mexican descent, but that was just too weird. Could there be some way that I was connected to this girl and didn't know it? Could it be that God Himself had gotten in on this, using me to help a distant relative find her peace? I don't know. When Rosa hears this, she won't believe it. No one will. I made sure to take a screenshot of the microfiche before I finished. I needed evidence when I talked to Mr. McCrank about this. And, of course, I would want to share it with Rosa.

I sat back from the table for a minute to just breathe. This is too crazy. "God, what's going on here?" I asked.

I still had to check the find-a-grave records on her. I had names and dates that would help me get going in the right direction. I did not know if the janitor was still living or if he had taken his life or died of natural causes, but if not, he would be at least in his mid to late eighties. I wasn't banking on that. I went back downstairs and signed in to use one of the computers to do the research. I typed in first Rosa Maria Rodriguez to see what I could find there. As I expected, there were over twelve hundred findings. I narrowed the search to 1972, and there I found her death notice, November 2, 1972. There was a brief mention of her death, with no details, and a mention of her remains being buried in the Catholic cemetery off Lohman Avenue. No services were mentioned. But there, at last, were her parents' names, Lorenzo and Rosa Rodriguez. I sat back from the table. I got up and walked around and had trouble breathing. All this together was just way too crazy. I was confused and lost. My mind was swirling with all that I had found out. I grabbed my jacket and headed out of the library without turning off the computer or signing out. I had to get some air.

So how does something like this happen? The exact same names. I had to find out who these people were. Was I related to this ghost girl? Could that be why she was crying out for help now? Was she hoping that a family member could help her join her family in the great beyond?

I remember Gideon in the book of Judges, in the Old Testament. Remember that story? "I am the least of my family from the least of my clan. How could I save Israel? Indeed, how could I, a school janitor, resolve a problem that had lasted for decades?

The Catholic cemetery mentioned was very nearby, less than a mile, so I walked out into the parking lot and got in my truck, and headed over to find the Rodriguez stones. I was quite familiar with the place; in fact, it had been church and cemetery to many of my relatives. It was not until my grandmother was baptized as an adult after the preaching of an evangelist that came into this area that we left the Catholic church and became non-denominational Christians. I had no disdain for my family who did not go along with us, but I feel, as my grandmother felt, that if one has been shone the truth about something, and especially something as important as the way of Christ, he or she had better follow it and leave others in God's hand who do not yet share that understanding.

It was dark as I pulled into the parking area of the cemetery. I left my headlight on to spread light, hoping it would help me find what I was looking for. The headlights gave the graveyard an other-worldly appearance. It was like being transported back in time. I reached over to my glove box and pulled out my flashlight. I used to carry one of those big jobs that use four D batteries, but now they've come out with this little job I use now. It just uses three AAA batteries, and it is super bright. The flashlight's beam will reach across this graveyard and beyond. Technology is making incredible gains in our day. It makes me wonder what is next. In this sacred place, the markers, for the most part, are very simple, white crosses, sometimes surrounded by little fences.

They are often decorated with flowers and rosaries, and other trinkets are placed on them. Often there are candles with saints pictured on them placed there that have been burned as a family member visited and prayed for their souls. The ground is not the lush green of eastern cemeteries but rather dry and brown; this is the desert. About a hundred feet in, coming from the church side of the cemetery, I find my cousin Jose's grave. He had died in a motorcycle accident at age seventeen. Near him were his mother and father, another Maria and Jose. These people were very special to me. The cemetery lot is perhaps three or four acres, not a small one but not the huge ones like the ones the Masons have on the south side of town. Across the road from the cemetery, the old Catholic church still stands, and many gather here even daily to celebrate the Mass. Just over to my left is the building they use for bingo and other church gatherings. It especially appeals to the older members of the church. It gives them something to do, encourages socializing and fellowship, and gives them a presence in the community.

I didn't know exactly where to look for the little girl's grave, but there had been a picture on the site of simple white crosses with her and her parents' names written on them and another brother or sister, along with her date of birth and date of death. I knew I would find it. All these events combined led me to this moment, and I knew that as surely as I had driven to this place of the dead, the marker would be there, and sure enough, there it was.

Only five markers down from my cousin. This was no coincidence. This girl had to be family. Her parents were buried on the other side of her, having died in their seventies. The girl's sisters and a brother were also buried there. They died young, one in her late twenties, another just over thirty, and the brother had died just this last year, at the age of fifty. I guess she was just a memory when he came along. What had happened that all these Rodriguez' had died so young? It seemed tragic to me, really. Not knowing these people, I couldn't be for sure, but I do know that our area has lost many young people to drugs, particularly methamphetamines. Then just the recklessness of youth. Who knows? I do know that I hate to see people die so young, without hardly even knowing what it is to live. Jesus died to show us a better way. Out here, in the ominous darkness of this holy place, I am reminded of how important my example and my voice are to sharing hope with those who seem to be lost in the chaos of this modern life. May God help me to remember to live my life with purpose. To be a light in a dark place.

My mom and dad were buried in Palomas, Mexico, which is not much bigger than the little village where Rosa is right now, but I had several other family members buried in this cemetery. How is it that I could have family members that I knew buried in the same area as these people, and I never took notice of them before? Well, I guess the answer to that one is easy. Where once people's lineage was very important to us, today we have become so transient that we hardly know the names of our grandparents, let alone those who went before them, or the names of cousins, aunts, and uncles who no longer live together with us in the same village. I wonder if we are not much poorer people for all we have gained by moving around the world chasing the almighty dollar. I found out recently that the name "Rodriguez" comes from "Rodrigo," the "EZ" meaning "son of." The roots of the name Rodrigo are very old but, when broken down from its compound form, mean something like "renown" and "powerful." So basically, I suppose, my name means something like the son of a famous and powerful man. Or famously powerful. Anyway, it's pretty cool. Who was the first "Rodrigo?" How did he get that name? What have I done to lift up or tear down that name? And I guess the bigger question is, what have we, the Rodriguez family, collectively done with it? When people hear the name Rodriguez, what do they think? Does it taste sweet on their tongues, or does it give them a bad taste? Remember those long ancestry lines in the Bible, so and so begat so and so who begat so and so who begat…I always wanted to rush through those. They were hard enough to say, and what did that have to do with my Christian walk anyway? Now it seems that God was showing us the importance of family and belonging to something far bigger than ourselves. When that thought came to me, I fell down on my knees right where I stood and repented, determining to do differently in whatever days I had left.

"Father," I said. "I am sorry that I, along with seemingly my whole generation and perhaps the generation before me, have forgotten the importance of family and belonging to one another. I see now that there is purpose in our belonging to one another. In a deeper sense, than I can realize even now, it holds us both accountable to one another and makes us realize the importance of the names that you have given us. Lord, I am a Rodriguez, and each generation, even each person bearing that name in a generation, decides just what that is going to mean.

Father, if you will empower me to do so, I will give heart and soul and mind and strength to make sure that, for my part, the name Rodriguez is a name that honors you. Help me to reconnect to my family as best I can and bring those still living to a clearer understanding of how important it is that we hold each other up as we travel the course that is set before us. I ask all this in Jesus' name. Amen."

I got up off my knees, with the lights of my truck still beaming across the graveyard. This little girl was family to me, somehow. And in some way that I did not know yet, I was going to help her find her peace and go home to join the Rodriguez' who had gone on before. Very good then. Okay. That was settled. I had work to do. I headed back carefully through that holy place and hopped back in my truck. I had left the door open the entire time, but it was okay. I had a good strong battery with 850 cold cranking amps that kicked it right off. I had just gotten a new battery last year. I spent the extra money and bought an Interstate battery, and so far, I did not regret it. The streets of La Plata were relatively quiet as I navigated out of town to our humble home in the Village of Dona Ana. It looked odd to drive in and not see the home lights burning. I pulled up and parked on our gravel drive. I was pretty hungry by now and looking forward to scratching something up for a nighttime snack. My wonderful Lottaburger was just a distant memory. I had in mind a bologna, cheese, and lettuce sandwich with mayonnaise sprinkled with salt and pepper. I might even add a pickle or two. If it was late summer, I would definitely add a couple of slices of ripe red tomatoes, but alas, summer was past and gone. O, well, this sandwich and a cold glass of milk to wash it down would settle my stomach's growling and set me up for a good night's sleep. I know you are thinking, "How can this dude eat with all these things going on in his life?" Honestly, I don't know. I always have been able to eat and sleep pretty well, no matter what's going on. Right now, I was not feeling like the exception. I went inside and hit the lights, and began the wonderful process of building my sandwich masterpiece. I kicked open the refrigerator and got out the milk and mayonnaise, the pickles and lettuce, the bologna and cheese, and then closed the frig up nice and tight. I wheeled around and grabbed the loaf of white bread that was on the counter. I know that lots of people eat only wheat bread these days, but I was raised on white bread, and I've never made the transition. To each his own, I guess. After I got everything lined up, I pulled out my cell and gave Rosa a call.

I put her on speaker, so I could go ahead and eat while we talked. I know it is not the best of manners, but I was hungry, and I really wanted to hear about Rosa's day and the health of her sister before I went to bed for the night. After three rings, I was surprised to hear my sister-in-law Maria's voice.

"Hello, Larry, is that you?" She asked.

Stunned, I held the phone speechless for a minute.

She tried again. "Hello, Larry, is that you? It says right here on Rosa's phone that it is you, Larry. Don't be trying to pull tricks on me." I could hear my wife laughing in the background.

"What…uhh, what?" That was all I could get out.

Suddenly my wife was on the line. "Larry, did you hear that? It's Maria! Larry, she's okay! She's been up around since sometime about an hour ago. I wanted to call you and tell you, but I knew that you were very busy at work, and I decided to wait and let you hear her for yourself. Lorenzo, It's a miracle! Our God has done it again!" She was almost shouting into the telephone.

"Rosa, Honey, slow down. I want to hear all about it. Give me the details!" I said, and even as I did, I heard her and her sister, and it sounded like several others laughing and shouting and praising God.

"Larry, this is no coincidence. This is a God thing! Not more than an hour ago, Maria was still weak on her bed. There may have been some small improvement throughout the day; I don't know. It might have been wishful thinking on my part. But then, Larry, it was like all of a sudden, she opened her eyes and threw off her covers. She sat up and then, just like that, she got up! I had been at her side all day, except to fix myself some lunch and bring her a little soup that I struggled to get her to take even a little off. Then around, I guess, about seven, I was looking for something to read in the magazine basket they have over by the couch. I thought maybe I could read out loud to her and pass the time. It was then that she stood up." I heard movement and turned around, and there she stood." I could see and hear laughter again in the background. I guess they were enjoying her retelling as much as I was. "Larry, I didn't know what to do. My first instinct was to tell her to sit back down before she hurt herself, but Larry, Lorenzo, she walked right over to me and gave me the biggest hug! She's healed, Baby! God has done this, and it is marvelous in our eyes. Larry, this is a God thing! Were you praying for my sister? Did God use your prayers to restore her heart?" She asked.

"Honey," I said. Tears were choking me as I tried to speak. "Honey, this is entirely a God thing! Give him all the glory and praise. It is not my faith but God's power that has restored your sister and made her whole! Amazing! What a mighty God we serve!" I am glad I was alone at that moment. Tears were rolling down my cheeks. I couldn't wipe them away fast enough, so I just let them come. How much this meant to my wife cannot be expressed in words. What it meant to me as a faith builder cannot be registered. I was in complete awe. I know that a lot of people might blow this whole thing off as a result of some medication or fortune, but I know that God did this, and I will not be quiet about it! I remembered the story of the lame man in the book of Acts in the New Testament who was healed. Peter said, "I have no silver or gold, but what I have I give to you; in the name of Jesus Christ of Nazareth, stand up and walk." Later, in Chapter four, Peter said, "…This man is standing before you in good health by the name of Jesus Christ of Nazareth, whom you crucified, whom God raised from the dead."

I was reminded then in a powerful way that the same power that raised Jesus from the grave lives in us, as a popular Christian song says. "Jesus Christ is the same, yesterday, today, and forever," the book of Hebrews says.

My wife brought me back from my revelry. "Honey? Are you still there?" She asked.

"Yes, Yes, Baby, I'm still here. Don't we have a wonderful God? I am so happy for you and your sister, Maria. Tell her I said that," I responded back.

"O, you just told her. I have you on speaker phone," she said.

Maria chimed in. "Lorenzo, thank you for your prayers! It is amazing what God can do. I was just lying there on the recliner, with no energy at all, and then it was like light pouring through me. I had the strongest impression that I should get up. I said in my mind, "But I can't get up. I am very sick." Then the voice said in my mind, or out loud, I do not know. In the name of Jesus Christ of Nazareth, get up!" I threw the covers off, and I lowered the leg rest on the recliner. I sat my feet on the floor and felt the power come into them, and, Larry, I stood up. I felt stronger than before I had my heart attacked. Rosa was there near me, and I walked over and gave her a giant bear hug! Lorenzo, there has never been a day like this in my life. I feel God's pleasure coursing through me, even now!" I could hear rustling and knew that Rosa and Maria were hugging again, and there were others there, shouting out, and it sounded like slapping high fives or something.

"Larry, honey, I guess I'll get off with you now. There is so much celebrating going on here that I can hardly hear you, but I love you, Baby. I'll talk to you tomorrow. Maybe then you can update me on what's going on at your school. Sweetheart, God is on the move! He will resolve your issue at Patton just as he has done mighty things here tonight. I love you!" She held the phone out from her ear, and several people at once shouted: "We love you, Lorenzo! You praying man of God, you!" and then, just like that, we lost the connection. The call was lost, the phone read.

Retry? I thought about calling back but couldn't think of a better ending than that.

Except now I really had something to think about. Those people, my people, were giving me credit for praying for the healing of my sister-in-law. I didn't deserve that. It is all grace, all the time. All I did, was the same as so many others were doing, was ask God to do what only God can do, and he did it. That makes it an all of him and none of me, kind of thing. Still, it made me wonder. "God, are you choosing me as a conduit through which you are going to work at this time? If so, why me? Don't get me wrong. There is nothing in the world that I want more than to be in harmony with your will, but who am I, God?" And then, after pausing and reflecting, I continued: "Lord, whatever you want, it is my honor to serve you, my God and my King."

I said no more. I sat there, alone in my house, and I ate my sandwich and drank my milk. It was delicious. I cleaned up after myself and went into the bathroom, where I showered and got ready for bed. Kneeling beside my bed, alone in our small but comfortable house, I prayed: "Thank you." I got off my knees and crawled into bed. I was immediately asleep.

Chapter 17

It was Friday morning. Halloween. Today, I knew it would be a crazy day at school. The kids would be wired for the fun they intended or wished for tonight. Monday, after eating all that candy, well, if I were a teacher that would be a day I would think about calling in. The sugar rush those babies would be on. Well, it's better to take one day at a time. Since Rosa was in Chihuahua and I was at the house all by myself, you'd think, well, maybe he will sleep in or turn on some loud music to get his blood pumping. But no. I got up at the same time as usual and took care of the necessary bodily functions. After I got my pearly whites brushed and beard shaved, I got in the shower and took a nice hot shower. The water felt good, waking me up and giving me that fresh feeling that I needed to power through a Friday. When the day was over, I'd come home and pack a few things and head down to the bus station. I couldn't wait to see Rosa and her sister, Maria. Seeing everybody healthy and blessed. I really had something to look forward to. And now that I knew more about this girl, I couldn't wait to share my possible family connection with Mr. McCrank this morning. He might think I was stretching things a bit, and I might be, but I don't think so. At any rate, we are all related somehow, and this little girl wanted me to help her. If we wondered what these recent goings on were all about, that note to Mrs. Douglass on her office window cleared that up for us. Too crazy. I don't know how the stuff in Mrs. Monte's classroom fits into all this, but the T.V. screen in Mr. Jackson's room that Mr. Rigsby saw certainly seemed to fit with someone crying out for help.

I stepped out of the shower and toweled off. All these things were running through my mind, and I still wasn't even dressed yet! The mind is hard to keep up with sometimes. Going into my bedroom, I got dressed, and then, as I was putting on my boots, I realized that I didn't want to go into all of today's business without a clear path for God to work through me and in me today. I bowed my head, right there, sitting on the edge of my bed.

"Lord, thank you for a new day. Thank you for the good news that Maria's health was restored yesterday. You are an awesome God! Thank you. I ask your blessings on Rosa and her family today. Give them a strong sense of your presence with them. Father, help me to do what I need to do today and to do it with joy in my heart. Empower me with your Spirit today so that I will bring you glory, doing only what you would do through me. Who am I to have such a privilege? Yet, here I am, your servant. Lord, I ask all this and give you praise in Jesus' name, amen."

When I had finished praying, I finished putting on my boots and headed quickly out to the truck. I would get some coffee in the lounge, and I have a few of those healthy crunch bars in my closet. I would just grab a couple of those and then maybe get a cafeteria lunch today. Though I rarely ate the school lunches, preferring to make my own, they were fairly priced and weren't bad, usually. Besides, I was so wired to get this day started and to share my news with Mr. McCrank and Mrs. Douglass, and Mr. Jackson. Especially the news about my wife's sister with Mr. Jackson. He was such a man of God, and I knew he would want to know what had happened and how God had worked in Maria's life.

When I pulled up to the school, I could see that, as often is the case, Mr. McCrank was already there. I grabbed my jacket and headed inside. I usually throw my jacket in the seat when I am driving. I don't like that bundled-up feeling I get once I put the seat belt on. Anyway, I pulled it on and hurried inside. Mr. McCrank was standing at the door waiting for me.

"Morning, Rodriguez. What's going on with you this morning? How's your wife's sister?" He asked.

"Good morning, Mr. McCrank. Fine, I'm fine. How are you?" I asked.

"It's Friday, Larry. You know how it is. Now tell me about your wife's sister. Is she doing any better?" He asked again.

"O yes, sir. She is. Mr. McCrank, I can't say it any other way. Mr. McCrank, God broke in on that situation; that's how our preacher would say it. She is healed!" He looked stunned and also was smiling to beat the band.

"Why, that's wonderful, Larry! What in the world happened?" He asked.

It's like I said, Mr. McCrank. God broke in. She was not doing well at all when I talked to my wife at lunch yesterday. And then, when I called last night, Rosa told me just all of a sudden, her sister got up off her sick bed. I talked to her sister, Maria, about it. She said it was like God told her to get up. She threw her legs off the couch where she had been lying, and she felt the strength come back into her body. She is healed, Mr. McCrank. This is nothing but a God thing, and all I can say is praise the Lord!" I said back like I was preaching from the church pulpit.

Mr. McCrank was a little taken aback by all I had to say. It was like he had to catch his breath from the force of my announcement. Then he said, "You know, Larry, I have believed in God all my life, I guess. There have been times, especially when I was in the Navy and I saw hard things, that I wondered why God was seemingly holding back. Where is God when people suffer and when bad things happen? I honestly don't know the answer to all those questions. But despite all that, I know somewhere deep inside myself that there are spiritual forces at work around us. We have certainly seen it lately here at this school, and then when I hear stories like this one of your sister-in-law being healed, I just have to join you in saying, "praise the Lord!" This is no doubt a "God thing," as you say.

"Thanks for allowing me to share my joy with you. I am glad that we are beginning to have a deeper sense of the spiritual world, even if it has taken a ghost girl to show us and help us get there," I said.

"Speaking of our ghost girl, did you get to go by the library and find anything else out about her? He asked.

"O, yes, sir, did I ever?" I said back energetically. It turns out that I may even be related to this girl. She is a Rodriguez, after all."

Mr. McCrank's eyebrows rose. "What?" He asked.

I laughed at his expression. "Yes, sir. Well, they are not closely related, but some of my people are buried near her people in the Catholic cemetery. They have very similar names. I, I don't have the facts in hand yet, but I think there is a real good chance we are related and, well, you know what I think, sir?

"What's that, Rodriguez? He asked. His old Navy attitude is showing itself.

"Well, sir, I think that my being one of the ones trying to solve this mystery and help this girl is another 'God thing,' sir." I watched his expression to see if he thought I might have finally gone off my rocker.

Instead, he took a moment, and then he said, "Who knows, Larry? Who knows? After all this, it wouldn't surprise me one bit." He used his hand to push back his thinning hair. "Larry, we now know this girl's name and family. We even know what she looks like. We are pretty sure that she is trapped here or staying here for some reason. We don't know what happened to Lee Goodland. As far as I can tell, he left here on that fateful night without a trace. Could it be that his disappearance and her staying here are connected in some way?"

I looked at Mr. McCrank with a dumbfounded look on my face, I'm sure. "Wow, sir, you really have been thinking this thing through. I don't know if you are right or not, but that could sure make sense. Maybe the girl knows where he is, or maybe she wants to find him," I said.

"Okay. That could be so, but if he were dead, as she is, then shouldn't they know that? I mean, I don't know. Do the dead hang out with each other or at least have some knowledge of who is dead? Those are crazy questions, I know. And to the other possibility, if she wanted to get a message to him or find him or whatever, why would she want to do that?" He asked.

We left that conversation unfinished. Not that we had an answer, really, anyway, but Mr. McCrank got a call on his cell. After he had talked a minute or so, he looked up from his conversation and mouthed, "I'll talk to you later," so I headed on down to the janitor's closet to get my day going. We still had to figure out what became of Lee Goodland. Was his wife still alive? I can't remember if Mr. McCrank told me anything about that. So many things are going on that I can't keep up with it all. But if she is still alive, she would be the obvious place to begin looking. If not, then maybe they had kids who would know something. All this was rumbling through my mind as I unlocked the doors of teachers who would not be here today. Since it is Halloween, the kids will be wired, some in costumes, though they are not supposed to wear the really creepy ones or those that have weapons with their costumes. Even though they know that Ms. David will still have to have a couple of parents bring a change of clothes for their kids or, if they are not available, have the kids go down to the nurse who has a small clothing bank to meet various needs. Usually, it's a kid who gets sick or spills milk on themselves at lunch, but having the wrong clothes on would also fit the bill. Over time, they have thought through many of the things these middle school kids can throw at them. That being said, they never cease to amaze me with the new situations they get into that need to be resolved. I'm sure I was never like that. Was I? In my case, my memory seems to be working in my favor.

That makes me think of something. Memory is always focused on the past. What has happened, either that actually happened or what we remember happened. The mind often adapts the actuality of things to make them fit with either what we can tolerate or what we wish happened. I don't think we do this consciously. It has something to do with our survival skills development. I am not a philosopher, but I just wonder if maybe this ghost girl and this janitor that was here so long ago, if maybe they are what we remember them to be. If our memory of them changed or the way we think of them, would they change in the substance of who they are? If it is true that we live, that is, our spiritual lives, forever, do our spirits, the essence of what we are, do they continue to change or become stagnant and permanent after we die? I don't know. Where do these thoughts come from, anyway? I really need to keep my focus on my work and work harder. Much harder.

It was this thought process that found me in the lounge scrubbing the counter. The coffee spills always need to be wiped away, but someone had spilled, I don't know what, maybe some cottage cheese, on the counter, and they just sort of smeared it in their efforts to clean it off. Nasty. I first wiped what hadn't hardened off, and then I got some cleaner; there wasn't anything under the counter except for some window cleaner, for some reason, so I sprayed the area down good with it and then cleaned it off again. The window cleaner has chlorine in it, so that at least killed that old nasty milk smell that goes with bad cottage cheese. Don't try this at home. When I put the window cleaner away, I spied some S.O.S. pads. They looked like they had been in there half of forever, kind of lost back in the back, but they were just what I needed. I got one of those and wet it a bit and then scrubbed away the residue. Having done that, I noticed there was crud back behind the sink and was going at that when Mrs. Douglass came in after a hot morning cup of coffee on a cold morning. I heard someone come in, but I didn't even look up; I was kind of in the moment if you know what I mean. She watched me a minute and then said, "Morning, Larry. You seem to be really focused on your work this morning," with a laugh. Breathing a little hard from my efforts, I stopped a minute and looked up at her, and grinned. "Good morning, Mrs. Douglass. Yeah, I, well, someone spilled something kind of disgusting here yesterday, and I just needed to get this mess cleaned up before you, and other teachers come in here to get your morning coffee. I guess whoever did it must have been in a hurry or something. Anyway, it's cleaned up now. Let me get out of your way so you can get your coffee."

"Thanks, Larry. I appreciate finding everything clean and fresh. You always do such a good job. You're probably right about the mess. I wonder who left that on you. That wasn't cool." She said.

"No, not too cool, but no worries. It's all cleaned up now. How are you doing this morning? Everyone healthy and happy in the Douglass family this morning?" I asked.

"Yes, we are all healthy and happy, Larry. Thanks for asking. How about you and yours? Is all well in the Rodriguez household?" She asked.

"O Mrs. Douglass, if things were to get any better, I don't think I could stand it. I might just explode in heavenly praise," I said, smiling at her. "My wife has a sister that was very sick down in Mexico. She went down to be with her, knowing that she could even die if her health didn't take a turn. But then yesterday, the Lord came into that situation and kicked death in the teeth. I can just hear it saying, 'Not this time, Death!" She is up on her feet and healthier than when she fell sick. Mrs. Douglass, God is moving! He is not playing."

Mrs. Douglass was smiling at me, with eyes wide with wonder. "Wow! Larry, you ought to be a preacher! I haven't heard anything as powerful as what you just said, even from the pulpit, in a long time. I'm just tingling all over! Wow! Thanks for sharing that with me." She was wearing a black tee shirt and jeans; it was Friday and Halloween, after all. Her tee shirt read "Trick or Teach," printed on an orange pumpkin. She was wearing her red Ked sneakers and had her hair up in a pony. She had to be in her forties, maybe in her late forties, but she was still having fun as a teacher librarian. Those who feel they have a purpose in what they do, do it with more energy. You can tell that they love what they do. She continued, "Larry, I don't have time right now, but later maybe you can update me on anything else you have learned about our ghost girl?"

"As a matter of fact, I have found out lots of good stuff. I'll be glad to share it with you. In fact, I will see if I can get you and Mr. McCrank and Mr. Jackson all together, maybe at lunch or after school. I believe we are about to get this mystery figured out and maybe help our girl find her way home." I hadn't any more than finished saying that when I felt a cold chill come into the room. I could see Mrs. Douglass scrunch her shoulders and wrap her arms around herself. "Did you feel that? I asked.

"I sure did!" She exclaimed. "I think she liked what you just said. O wow! This is super cool! Some way to start Halloween. O, man. That was crazy! Hey. Let me get in there and get my coffee. I need to get warmed up and get to work. This is going to be a day, Mr. Rodriguez. It will be quite a day."

"Yes, ma'am, and somehow we are right in the middle of it. Okay, God. Okay, Ghost Girl. Let's get this party started," I said, using a line from one of the kids I often see on campus. His name is Edgar, and he is funny. Kids are always laughing around him. He is one of that ' life of the party types.

Mrs. Douglass got her coffee and then looked at her watch. "O my goodness, the bell is going to ring at any minute. I'll see you later, Larry. It is going to be some, mkday," she said as she turned and headed out of the lounge.

I spent the rest of the day working hard, cleaning in those tight spots that I often overlooked because the job of cleaning such a huge complex is daunting at times. I do the best I can, but, well, sometimes I just have to hit the main points and let the rest go. Today, however, since my mind had so many things to chew on, I just had to concentrate on my work. I scrubbed the bathrooms especially well and cleaned up better than I had in a long time around the dumpsters where the cafeteria throws all their excess.

As the end of the school day drew near, I took my post out along the front of the school, directing traffic. The temperature was cool, maybe low forties, with a slight breeze in the air, and I had my jacket zipped up tight. There were lots of parents even wearing masks of different creatures as they came to pick up their kids. Hopefully, the masks we wear don't reflect the person inside. I guess I'll stay with the mask I was born with for now. One day, the Bible says, we will be given glorified bodies. I guess that includes glorified faces? Well, I know that the day we see the face of Jesus, really see him face to face that will be the day. I just want to reflect on his glory. Jesus. I can't wait.

Anyway, with all the cones picked up, I headed back into the building. I put the cones in the closet and started my first rounds of picking up trash in the teachers' rooms. I saw Mr. Jackson and told him I was hoping he and I and Mr. McCrank and Mrs. Douglass could get together, maybe even today, before they all headed for home to talk about our ghost girl. I told him we had discovered some things that might be of interest to them. He seemed very interested and asked if Mr. Rigsby could get with us too.

"Sure, Mr. Jackson. That would be great. I guess he was the one to see the girl on the T.V. that day. Let me see if I can get Mr. McCrank and Mrs. Douglass in on this. I figure just a few minutes so we can get everyone updated and maybe come up with a game plan. I'll be back to let you know when and where," I said.

"Sounds great, Larry. See you soon," Mr. Jackson said. He paused, and then he said, "Hey, Larry. Thanks for taking the lead on this. God has raised you up for this, you know."

I looked at him a minute, nodded my head, and then I was off like a shot to get the others. I kind of felt like this thing was finally coming together. As I came around the corner, turning toward the library, I ran right into Mr. McCrank. Bam! Both of us staggered back, stunned for a moment, and then, in unison, we both started laughing. Kind of the crazy laughing you hear from people who have been dealing with too much stress.

"Mr. Rodriguez, I was just coming to find you. Sorry about that. Are you okay?" He said.

"Yes, sir. I think you might have knocked some sense into me, but I'm okay. Sorry, I came around the corner so quickly. I was hoping to run into you, but not quite like that," I said in response.

We both laughed again, and then I told him about talking with Mr. Jackson and that I was also hoping to get Mrs. Douglass in on this pow wow. Just as I said that, she came out the library door, all in a bustle. "What on earth? What was all that noise, and why are you two lying on the floor, of all places? She asked.

We were both laughing. "What can we say?" Mr. McCrank said. "As much work as there is around here, a man has got to rest when he can."

"Okay, boys," she said in response. I have more real work to finish before I go home. Have a nice rest."

"Wait, Mrs. Douglass, we all need to get together for a few minutes to talk about our special situation here," I said, making sure to mask what we needed to talk about from those who were not necessarily in the know. No reason to get others involved if it isn't necessary.

Mr. McCrank looked at me and then Mrs. Douglass. "Can you two meet me in my office in, say, ten minutes to discuss this issue?"

"Sure, boss," we said, almost in unison. He got up and straightened his pants legs, and dusted himself off. Taking one last look at me, a look that said, 'Hummph!' and then he headed up to his office.

I got up out on the floor myself and then said to Mrs. Douglass, "If we ever get to the bottom of this crazy business, I think I'll write a book about it and call it "Ghost Girl." Most people probably wouldn't believe it, calling it fiction, so I could write it just as it happened and sell it that way, maybe."

"You really should write that book, Larry, but you have the title all wrong. While it is true that we apparently have a ghost in this school that needs our help, this book is about the school janitor who solved the mystery and saved the day. Just look at that title in the bright lights: "The School Janitor, starring Larry Rodriguez." Now that's a book that would sell. People would snatch it off the shelves, kind of like my poetry books that keep falling on the floor, but different," she said, smiling.

"Okay, Okay, Mrs. Douglass. That's what we'll call it. I'll share my abundant wealth with all of you, and we can all retire and buy ourselves a remote island and live happily ever after. The end."

"See," she said, "your writing juices are getting all fired up already. See you in the funny papers."

"That's exactly where I'll be. See you after a while in Mr. McCrank's office." I hustled down the hall to finish my duties before the meeting. It would be very hard to concentrate on my work with so much swirling around in my head. Maybe I would imagine my book as I swept the halls and picked up trash. Crazy how you can complete huge projects in minutes in your mind that are almost impossible in real-time.

Chapter 18

At just past four pm, we met in Mr. McCrank's office. Mr. Jackson, Mrs. Douglass, Mr. McCrank, and myself. Mr. Jackson would fill Mr. Rigsby in as necessary. We needed a plan, and we felt like we were almost where we needed to be to devise one.

"Thanks for coming. I know you all have things to do or families to get home to, but you all know that some strange things are happening here at Patton, and we have to get to the bottom of it."

"Mr. McCrank, I'm sorry to interrupt you, but something happened in the library that you need to know about. I know you, and I found out who the little girl was and who the janitor was, but now, with what Mrs. Douglass can tell you, we may finally know what to do with this information," I said, looking a little sheepish under the eye of Mr. McCrank. He wasn't used to being interrupted.

"All right, then. What's this about, Mrs. Douglass? Have you got some new information to shed on the subject?"

Mrs. Douglass seemed to shrink a little with all the attention suddenly turned on her. "Uh, well, uh, I, there was a note left for me, apparently from the little girl that was killed here, our 'Ghost Girl'. I know this is super crazy, but maybe by now, nothing seems out of bounds. The girl asked for help in finding 'him'. I showed it to Larry, and we think the 'him' is the janitor from all those years ago who accidentally, the way I hear it, killed her. She wants to tell him that she is okay and that she wants him to go on living and not blame himself. I guess somehow, that is the reason that she is still here all these years later. She could not go on to be with her family until she cleared this up. With the Day of the Dead coming up in just a couple of days, I think that is the reason she is so urgent to get this cleared up so that she can join her family once and for all in the celebration." She looked over at me and continued: "I just thought of this last part after we talked, Larry. Do you think that makes sense? I mean, after all, the Dia de los Muertos is your heritage. We are just Anglos who have learned about it."

All eyes turned to me. The legend is, and I am not sure if I subscribe to it, that the dead come back to visit us on Dia de los Muertos. I am not sure if that is the only day when we die, and I guess we are talking about those who have been stuck here for one reason or another, can go over to join them or not, but that is a good theory. I'd say a very good theory."

"The man's name," Mr. McCrank said, "the janitor from back in the 1960s and 1970s, I mean, is Lee Goodland. He was the evening janitor here at Patton when the school was young. There is a picture of him in the old school annual. It seems that Mr. Goodland was a good man. Kept his head down and did his work.

He was a quiet man who was appreciated for his service but otherwise unknown, mostly, by the people who worked here back then. You know the type. They come, and they go. They do their job, so no one complains, but they don't make any waves, and so they are more of the backdrop rather than the show. We have them here at our school now. Wilson, Hernandez, Calderon, just to name a few.

We couldn't run this ship without them, and generations of kids have been trained by them. We'd be lost without them. I think our Mr. Goodland was that kind of man. And then, one night, everything changed for him. By some freak accident, his life went from a monotonous though peaceful existence to a living hell. He couldn't process it. It wrenched his gut and drove him away from everything he knew to only God knows where.

To my knowledge, no one, even today, knows where he is or even if he is still alive. If he is still alive, he has to be in his eighties, at least. Still, if he is still alive, and it seems our ghost girl thinks he is, then we are called together to help find him and deliver her message to him, or better still, have her tell him herself. Then, maybe, by the grace of God, the two of them can resolve this burden that has weighed them down for nearly fifty years, and, well, and then they and this school can finally be at peace. All of you know me, except maybe Mrs. Douglass, you've only been here a short time, but I can't pull any wool over the eyes of the rest of them. I have not been a religious man. It's not that I haven't believed in God. You can't be out on the sea, as I was in the Navy, and see and experience the things that I have and not believe in God. Still, in a way that I have never experienced before, I am seeing God at work here and through many of you. Between Mr. Jackson's continual spirit of joy and Larry's recent testimonies to me of how God has worked in his wife's sister's health," he turned and looked at me, "you'll have to ask him about it. It's a pretty fantastic story. On second thought, I'm sure he has already told you. Larry, you put the 'P' in proclaim, and now this little girl, who somehow, God is showing me that her place is with her family of which he is, shall we say, the Godfather." He looked at all of us, scanning our faces to see if we were with him. "Folks, we have got to get this done, and I believe and know that we will. And we need to have it done in the next two days! Dia de los Muertos is upon, right, Larry?"

Such a speech Mr. McCrank gave to us. None of us were expecting it, and when he called on me, I was a moment lighting back down to answer him. "Um, yes, sir! Our day of honoring our dead is upon us. Their spirits will be here soon. I never was all in on this whole Day of the Dead thing, other than just a sweet family tradition, but now, well, now, I think it must be true. The old people were not only quaint but right!" I said, with a conviction that I had never known. A conviction that surely came from God Himself.

"Okay then. Listen, all of you. I need your help to get this done. Can I count on you?" Mr. McCrank asked.

"Sir, I will do whatever you feel needs done," Mr. Jackson said.

"Me too!" Mrs. Douglass called out.

"Great! I need you. Mr. Jackson, I want you to find out where Mr. Goodland is, even if, even if we find him lying in a graveyard."

"Yes, sir, I'm on it."

"And Mrs. Douglass, it seems that this girl trusts you, somehow, maybe it's the female connection, I don't know, but I want you to talk to her. Tell her what we are doing to find Mr. Goodland. Ask her how we can help."

"Yes, sir, I can do that. It is pretty far out of my wheelhouse, but I'll do anything I can to help solve this mystery."

"Great. And Mr. Rodriguez, somehow, you are the hub of this whole thing. Maybe because of your connection, you know, janitor to janitor, or your spiritual connection and trust in God for purpose in things, I'm not sure. But I do believe that when we find Mr. Goodland, you will be our man to intercede with him."

Yes sir. I'd be honored to do that, Mr. McCrank. And Mr. McCrank, thanks for taking the lead on this. You were born to lead, sir, if you don't mind me saying so, sir."

"Hmmm," was all he said. I guess he felt like I was blowing smoke or was embarrassed by what I said. I don't know. Maybe I shouldn't have said it. But I sure meant it. What could it have been like to be under his leadership on a ship in the open waters? Confidence is the word that comes to mind. I guess if you have confidence in one's leadership, you'd be willing to follow them almost anywhere. That's kind of a Jesus thing, now that I think about it. "Anywhere with Jesus, I can safely go…" the old hymn sings. Lead on, Lord!

We broke out of our meeting, excited about getting to our assignments. I wanted to get to a phone and call Rosa and tell her what was going on here and find out how she and her sister were doing down in Chihuahua. My Rosa. If you only knew her, you would know why she keeps coming back into my mind, sort of like a spirit or ghost. Even when she is not with me, she is still there. I feel her presence with me. God, how I love that woman. Life is hard, and struggles are many, but how blest I am to have her with me through it all. How blessed I am.

"Rosa," I said from my cell phone. I had gone to the call room in the teacher's lounge to make the call. "Rosa, how are you doing, honey? How's your sister, Maria? I sure do miss you, baby. I can't wait to see you again." I said all this in one great blast of emotion.

"Well, how are you, Lorenzo? I miss you too, baby. I have so much to tell you, and by the sound of it, you have a lot to tell me also."

"You got that right, but you first. Is Maria still doing well?"

"Listen, Maria is doing so well, just like she never was sick. She is turning cartwheels all around me. I can't keep up with her. And guess what? You are not going to need to come down here this weekend. We are coming up to La Plata on the bus tomorrow morning! Maria felt so good, and she said it had been too long since she had been up to see us; she said she was not going to miss this chance now that her health was back. Honey, we are coming home!"

"Well, well, hallelujah! That's wonderful good news! How did this all come about?"

"It's the craziest thing. I mean, I came down here, praying my heart out that my sister would live. I couldn't bear the thought of not seeing her at least one more time. O me of little faith!

Now she is like a kid; I mean it, Larry. And you know what? It's like I have more life in me than I have had in so long. Honey, we went over to the family graveyard. We built an altar there, right on the spot, to honor our parents, brothers and sisters, our grandparents, and relatives from long ago. We built that altar and brought them bread and cookies and flowers. We sat among them and told them what we were going to do. That we were planning to come up and be with you on this holy day. Lorenzo, baby, it was like this peace came over both of us, and we looked at each other at the same time, tears streaming from our eyes, and we knew that God had given us this marvelous family connection. Larry, it was like we had their blessing in coming to be with you. Honey, there is a whole other world out there among the spirits, and somehow, at this time in our lives, our minds and hearts are finally being opened up to it. I don't ever want to lose it."

"No, no, we won't, Rosa. I feel so rich right now. I feel like I have been blessed and knew it, but now it is as if I am abounding more and more. He has anointed my head with oil. My cup overflows. Surely goodness and mercy shall follow me all the days of my life, and I will dwell in the house of the Lord forever." It was like God's psalms were just flowing out of this deep wellspring within my soul. Like I was a conduit of the spirit or something. I'm just a school janitor. I don't deserve this kind of blessing, this kind of joy.

Rosa came back through the phone line. "Honey, we are blessed. We are swimming in his mercy and grace right now, even in our birthday suits. He knows every spot and blemishes about us, and he loves us anyway. I love being known by him. He calls us by name. We hear his voice and follow him."

"Sounds good to me. Rosa, honey, I have to get back to work. As soon as I get the school house cleaned up, I am going to work with Mr. Jackson to see if we can find this Mr. Goodland, the janitor from way back when. We are going to help this ghost girl find her family and let this same peace that we have descend on both of them. I am not sure how all this is going to work out, but it is going down quickly! Dia de los Muertos is almost here, and we don't want anyone to miss it!"

'Okay, sweetheart. Get it done! As some folks say. Can't wait to see you. Tomorrow night!"

I'll come and pick you up. I'm sure Mr. McCrank won't mind if I take a few minutes to come to get you and your sister. He knows I'll get the building cleaned up. Okay, honey, I'm gone. See you soon."

"Bye, honey. I love you."

"I love you too." I ended the call and sighed. "How good. How good," I thought to myself.

I left the teacher's lounge and got busy sweeping the halls and picking up the classroom trash at the same time. I emptied pencil sharpeners and wiped down desks. I brought the vacuum and moved desks around, and took care of that in Mr. Jackson's room. His room is half carpet and half tile due to it having once been two different rooms. Besides his room, the library and office are the only other places that I have to vacuum. Mr. Jackson was in his room working away on some papers when I came in.

"Hey, Larry," He said. "I am going to get this test graded and entered, and then I plan on begin searching from Mr. Lee Goodland. I know we can find him. I just hope he's still alive and accessible. This whole thing is getting pretty exciting, don't you think?"

"Sure do, Mr. Jackson. Will it be okay if I knock this vacuuming out right quick? It will only take a minute."

Sure, Larry, I'm just grading tests. I have a score sheet, and after I have done a few, I don't even need that. A lot of the work I do can be kind of mindless, but it just has to be done."

"Okay. Thanks, Mr. Jackson. I know what you mean. I'll get right to some of that mindless work right now." I fired up the vacuum and got busy.

When I finished in Mr. Jackson's room, I headed out of there and on to the library. Might as well do that vacuuming while I was at it.

I found Mrs. Douglass in her library. She was talking to someone when I went in. I didn't think anything of it. I didn't see anyone else, but I figured there must be a teacher in the copy room, which was just past the main counter. She had her attention turned in that direction anyway, so I just came in quietly and started to empty the trash cans and her pencil sharpener. Then she saw me out of the corner of her eye, and just kind of waved me on in.

"Maria, you know Larry here. He is also trying to help us find Mr. Goodland. We are going to do our best to have him to you by or before the Day of the Dead. Sorry, it has taken us so long to understand what you needed. We can be kind of slow sometimes."

It took me a minute, and then I realized that she was talking to our ghost girl.

"Uh, hello, Maria. It looks like you and I might be family on down the line. I know that Dia de Los Muertos is coming up, and I think that this is your shot at clearing things up with Mr. Goodland and joining your family. We are going to do everything we can to see that that happens," I said, looking at Mrs. Douglass for approval. Was this girl really there, and was Mrs. Douglass, were we, really communicating with her? I waited a moment for a response. Nothing.

"Well," I continued. "I just need to get this carpet vacuumed up really quick if that's okay, and I'll get out of you ladies' way."

"Sure, that will be fine, Larry. Are you going down to Mr. Jackson's room later to see what he finds out?"

Yes ma'am. I just came from there, but when I get my work done, I'll swing by to see what he has found out. Maybe I'll see you down there."

"Sounds good. Hey, Maria? Maybe you will want to head down there with us too to see what we can see."

There was a chill that went up our backs at the same time; I could see it in Mrs. Douglass' eyes.

"Creepy cool," she said, looking at me.

"I'll say," I said and headed on out to complete the rest of my duties.

I looked at my watch to check the time when I finished vacuuming the office and hauling out the three bags of shredded paper. They sure go through lots of paper at this school. Anyway, the time was 1730 hours exactly. Even though I was never in the military, military time makes so much more sense than civilian time. There are no do-overs. It is only 1730 one time a day, but there are two 530s on civilian time. We use a.m. and p.m. to distinguish them from each other, but how much simpler to just use the twenty-four-hour system. That's all I'm saying.

Down in Mr. Jackson's classroom, I could hear the excited talk. I hurried to see what was going on. Mr. McCrank and Mrs. Douglass had joined him, and they all had light in their eyes. When I stepped in the door, they all said, almost at the same time, "We found him! We found him! Mr. Goodland is alive!"

Mr. Jackson picked it up. "Mr. Rodriguez, Mr. Goodland is not only alive, but he lives in La Luz. We can be at his house in an hour and a half. I have a number for him here and everything. We were just about to call him, but thinking about it, I think you ought to be the one to talk to him. You know 'Janitor Speak' as it were. What do you say, Mr. Rodriguez? Will you make the call?

All eyes were on me, and I knew then that this was why I had been a part of this all along. It was up to me to bring him in. I knew 'Janitor Speak' after all. "Okay," I said. "Let's get this party started."

"We can use my cell phone if that's okay," Mr. Jackson offered.

Mr. McCrank said, "Well, thank you, Mr. Jackson, but I think, just in case he has caller ID, we ought to call from the office phone. He might be more inclined to answer it if it was from a source he knew."

"Yeah, or not," said Mrs. Douglass. "The man has been afraid of this ghost of his past for nearly fifty years. How is he going to feel when he sees Patton Middle School come up on his caller ID?"

"Well, that's a good question," Mr. McCrank said, "but I guess it is a chance I'm willing to take. Maybe he will feel some sense of duty to answer to call."

"Let's hope so," Mr. Jackson said, and we all got up and headed on down toward the office.

"Vamanos."

We all looked at each other. It was quiet for a minute. It was obvious that we all heard that word and that it was not any of us who said it. We looked back and forth toward one another, and then we all just broke out laughing.

"Si, vamanos," I said. "Come on, Maria. Let's get this done."

In the office, we gathered around the phone like it was a fire pit. I held the phone in my hand, trembling a little. "What, exactly, am I going to say? I asked.

Mr. Jackson said, "Hold on a minute, Larry. Let's pray about juthis first." We all bowed our heads in anticipation of Mr. Jackson's prayer, but it was Mr. McCrank that prayed.

"Lord, we are gathered here in your name, hoping to help a little girl and an old man find peace. We feel like this is something that you have called us together to do, but we can't do it without you. Please give Larry the words he needs to say to bring Mr. Goodland in. May they and we, here at Patton Middle School, have peace at last. I ask in the name of your son, Jesus Christ. Amen."

Pleased to hear my boss pray and encourage, I brought the phone to my ear and dialed the number. As an afterthought, I reached up and pushed the speaker button.

"Hello?" Came the reply on the other end of the line.

"Hello. I'd like to speak to Mr. Lee Goodland, please."

"My name is John; I am Mr. Goodland's caregiver. I'm afraid he's napping right now. Can I take your name and have him call you back when he wakes up?" He asked.

"Um, this is Larry Rodriguez. I am the day janitor at Patton Middle School. Mr. Goodland used to work here many years ago. Mr. Goodland doesn't know me, but I have some important news for him and…."

"Hold on, Mr. Rodriguez. He's waking up. Let me get him some water and see if he needs anything, and then I'll tell him who's on the line. I'd say he'd be glad to talk to you. He gets mighty lonesome sometimes.

We all waited as we heard various sounds through the telephone, no doubt the getting of water and maybe even Mr. Goodland being walked to the bathroom and back. I guess I was beginning to think that they forgot we were waiting on the phone when I heard John tell Mr. Goodland about the phone call.

"Who did you say? Larry? From Patton Junior High? I used to work there; did you know it? What's he want? I'm sure I cleaned those toilet stalls. I always do a good job."

"Yes, sir. I'm sure you do. I don't think you're in trouble, Mr. Goodland. The man said he had some important news for you."

"Oh, well, why didn't you say so?"

We heard the rustling of some sort and then his voice on the phone.

"Hello? Who is this? John says you have some important news for me."

I caught my breath and said, "Mr. Goodland. Is this Mr. Lee Goodland?"

"That's who you called. What do you want?"

"Sir, this is Larry Rodriguez. I am the day janitor at Patton Middle School in La Plata."

"I thought it was Patton Junior High. You said the one in La Plata, right? That's the one I work at. I don't remember you." He was getting a bit mixed up, but I thought I better stay in the present.

"Sir, when you worked here, there was a terrible accident, do you remember?"

There was a long pause. I could almost see the tumblers turning in his mind. "Ohhh, yes, I do. It was a terrible accident. I don't know what happened exactly, but there was a little girl that got caught behind the bleachers. We had just gotten these new-fangled power bleachers. I thought we just had to have them. I had no idea there would be a little girl behind them when I closed them up after the ballgame. I felt terrible, but it wasn't my fault. The Voice thought otherwise and just wouldn't quit. I couldn't get the noise out of my head. I ran away from there, Mr. Rodriguez. I had to. I'm sorry it happened, but it wasn't my fault."

Just then, John took the receiver from Mr. Goodland. "Hey, mister. I don't know what this is about, but you are upsetting Mr. Goodland. I am going to have to let you go and see if I can get him calmed down."

I could just see him moving that phone down to its cradle.

"Hold on! Wait, John. Let me explain."

He lifted the receiver back up to his ear. "Okay, but you better make it good."

"Thank you," I said. "John, Mr. Goodland was involved in a terrible accident here at Patton almost fifty years ago. It was an accident, but I know that he never got peace from that knowledge. I know that he was haunted by accident, and that is why he just disappeared for all these years. We did not know for sure if he was still alive, but we had to give it a try. John, we have a plan to finally give Mr. Goodland the peace he needs and let him live out the rest of his life, however long that is, without guilt from what happened. That's all we want, but we need Mr. Goodland to come to La Plata and Patton Middle School to make that happen."

"Ummm, how is that going to help?" he asked.

"Okay, John. You are just going to have to trust me on this. I have the assistant principal here with me right now, and he is telling me that we will pay for your gas and food and even put you and Mr. Goodland up for the night if you come over."

He hesitated, and I could almost see the wheels turning. "Look, you said that Mr. Goodland needed company. That he was bored. This will give him a plan for a day or two and maybe even bring about peace for him that anybody would need, especially an old man in the winter of his life. What do you say?"

"Alright, I'll bring him. I suppose it can't hurt. When would be the best time?"

"Saturday morning. Will that work for you?"

"Okay. Let me check his calendar. Sometimes we have doctor's appointments. No, No, we are clear. What time is after school? Around nine a.m.?"

"Yes, perfect. Nine a.m. Saturday. And don't worry about the gas and meals. And lodging if you want to stay the night. Thank you, John. Be sure to tell Mr. Goodland, "thank you."

"I will. I hope you don't mind me saying this, but this is kind of weird, Mr. Rodriguez. I hope we don't live to regret this."

"No, sir. You won't. Thanks again, and see you then." I hung up the phone. There was a collective sigh of relief that sounded like it came from more than just the four of us in the room.

"Maria," Mrs. Douglass said. "We are about to get this done. Saturday will be here before you know it. If this all works out right, you are going to get this mess cleared up and be on your way to family and celebration!"

There was a slight breeze that passed through Mr. McCrank's office. I know that sounds crazy and unbelievable, but there were four of us there that experienced it. That's all I'm saying.

So, we are going to meet with Mr. Goodland. We obviously have our ghost girl hanging tight with us as an ally rather than a grievance, and we are all keyed into what is going on, so none of us feels like we are on our own.

We all sort of broke up from there. I got back to cleaning, and Mr. McCrank stayed in his office working on what administration works on, Mr. Jackson headed back to his room, and Mrs. Douglass headed out to her SUV, saying she had kids to pick up. It all looked like we were going back to live as usual, but that was anything but the case. It seems like most of our lives; we live looking like one thing while a whole different dynamic is happening on the inside.

Chapter 19

That night, well, I sure wasn't going to sleep very well with all the things going on in my head. You know the voices that continually occupy your mind every waking hour. Sometimes it's just the last song you heard on the radio, so "Be careful little ears what you hear," as the little children's song says. I personally have been led from happy to miserable to sad or vice versa just by the power of a song. Someone has said, "The man you feed is the man who will lead."

My mind was full of the things going on at school that would soon, it seemed, come to some kind of conclusion, and my wife and her sister coming up tomorrow (I could hardly wait to see my wife!), and even just then I remembered that this was Halloween night! The kids at school will be wired after eating all that candy. And they will have it with them, and there will be papers all over everywhere. Oh, well. Un dia a la vez. That is not a big deal out in Dona Ana, where Rosa and I live. A few kids would come around to ask for Trick or Treats. With that in mind, I needed to stop by the Save Mart and pick up a bag of candy, just in case I couldn't scrounge up something at the house. And while there, I guess picking up some flowers for Rosa's return would be nice. I would have them on the table for her to see when she came in with her sister. Only this time, I would get red ones! Those white ones sure didn't go over very well. That reminds me that I need to throw them out when I get home. They are all laid over now and would not be a good reminder.

I pulled into the Save Mart. It was only six thirty or so, 1830 hours in military time. Anyway, it was much earlier than last time. I went in through the automatic door and hustled back to the candy aisle. I picked up one of those bags of candy that had six or seven different kinds of chocolate candy bars in them. You really can't go wrong with chocolate.

As I came up to the counter, there were the red roses I was hoping for, and there was the same girl that sold me the flowers last time. I picked out the freshest of the bouquets of roses, put them in the little bag provided to keep them from making a mess, and laid them and the candy on the counter. The girl ran the candy through, and as she was scanning the flowers, she looked up and recognized me. She still had that name tag on. "Jenny," it read. I would have remembered anyway. Things were so strange last time, and she even called after me to offer me a ride home when her dad came to pick her up. She might be a confused high school girl, but down deep, she was just a good person.

"Hey, you're the guy who bought the mysterious white flowers from me recently. Still don't know where those came from. You sure look a lot better tonight than you did the other day. Are you feeling better?"

"Hey, well, sure. I feel fine. I really don't know what was going on the other night. I sure am glad you have red roses tonight. My wife is coming home tomorrow, and I want to have them welcome her home."

"Your wife sure is a lucky woman. You are buying her flowers all the time; it seems like to me. What woman wouldn't be happy about that? My boyfriends…well, let's just say they have never been so thoughtful. But you know what? My birthday is Saturday, and my mom and dad are taking me to the Dripping Springs Nature Area. We love to go up there and hike the trails and take pictures of all the natural beauty. It just seems like God is in those mountains, you know what I mean? I love walking up to those old horse stables and where the sanitorium used to be. But I really like Hermit's Cave. Have you been there?"

"Sure. I love that place, and the Hermit's Cave is my favorite too. Did you know the hermit was a priest or monk?"

"Yeah, and somebody killed him. Stabbed him in the back. He had a fire going every day. His friends down in town watched for it to make sure he was okay. One day they didn't see any smoke coming from his fire. When they went up to check on him, they found him dead, face down with a knife in his back. You know, they say his ghost still shows up there sometimes. Do you think that is true?"

"Hmmm. Until recently, I would have said no, but now I am not so sure. Where ever he is, I hope he is at peace."

"Amen! You know, at night, this place can get pretty quiet at times. Not many people shop here now with Wal-Mart just down the road. Still, we are convenient to the locals, especially if they just need to pick up a few things. And then, there are those who were shopping here long before Wal-Mart came. They will be loyal until they die, I suppose. But they are getting older. When they are gone, I suppose this store will be another victim, and only the spirits of the past will walk these isles looking for bread or cheese."

"Jenny, you are one deep thinker. I bet your teachers love having you in class."

"Me? No. I don't really talk in class. I leave that to the school girls and book worms. I do think about what they say, though, and mull the thoughts around in my mind. It helps me understand things. Hey, mister, most people just come in here and get what they need, and then they're gone. They might talk about the weather or ask me how I'm doing; you know how people do. But it seems to me that you see me as a person. I appreciate that."

I shook my head. "Well, you are a person, Jenny. I very intelligent and thoughtful person, it seems to me."

Thanks, mister. Hey, I see from your work shirt that your name is Larry?"

"Oh yeah, I'm sorry. My name is Larry Rodriguez. I just live up here in Dona Ana. I work as a janitor at Patton Middle School. It's good to meet you, Jenny. I better be getting on up the road. I want to have everything ready for my wife when she comes home. She is bringing her sister, Maria, with her from Chihuahua. I've got to get the guest room ready."

"Okay, Larry. Thanks for stopping in. I hope your wife enjoys those flowers. Happy Halloween!"

"Yeah, happy Halloween to you, Jenny!"

With that, I was out the door and headed home.

Chapter 20

The house was empty and lonely when I pulled into our gravel drive. This place, as nice and quiet as it is out here in the country, with a view of the mountains all around, was just a house without my Rosa. I knew she would be with me by this time tomorrow, praise God, but I sure would have loved to see her come out to greet me as I pulled in. If she were here with me right now, I would wrap my arms around her and look here at the great panorama that God has painted all around us. Just here to the west is Picacho Peak, a long extinct volcano.

To the north are the Robledo Mountains and the Dona Ana Mountains. The former has prehistoric dinosaur tracks; the latter has a marvelous window rock and rocks at its base that can be walked around in like a maze. To the south are the Tres Hermanas, or Three Sister Mountains. Kilbourne Hole is there. An ancient meteor strike site. To the east are the Organ Mountains. Given that name because they reminded early travelers of church organs.

These mountains form the tail end of the great Rocky Mountains. From the San Augustin Pass, where the mountain is crossed to the east, one can see the awesome expanse of the Tularosa Basin. The Trinity Site is to the north, the site of the first atomic bomb blast, and to the south is the Small Missile Range. On a clear day, one can witness the army testing various missiles and bombs. It's pretty cool. Just across to desert another fifty miles are the great White Sands, Holloman Air Force Base, the Sacramento Mountains, Alamogordo, the International Space Museum, and Sun Spot, where there are observatories high up on the mountain. This is an enchanted land, and by God's grace, we live here! All that is missing to make my heart full is my sweet Rosa. God willing, I can live out my vision with her here with me as soon as tomorrow night! Hope is a glorious thing.

Going on inside, I fixed myself a bite to eat, a simple meal of beans and tortillas. Frijoles. Another simple yet beautiful gift from God. Gracias, Dios. Gracias. I went into our spare bedroom. It had been the kids' room when they were still here with us. I will not spend much time speaking of them. We are still in constant contact and get along nicely. Our love for them has never been stronger, but if I let myself go very far down that path, I become overwhelmed with emotion and become basically useless. For those of you with children, you know where I'm coming from. They are my heart. They are my life. Even now, after being gone from home for many years…When Rosa and I are with our children, one boy, and two girls, we always have a wonderful reunion. But honestly, I must guard my heart. I don't even look them in the eyes most of the time. Why? Because when I look into their eyes, I see the little boy and little girls that used to run around our feet and occupy our every waking moment. The eyes are the window to the soul. Though we age and our bodies change, our eyes remain the same. The same eyes that looked up to me with arms outstretched still look at me and say 'Dad' today. I can hardly speak of it without losing myself in tears. This is their room. It will always be their room. But Maria is coming tomorrow, and for a time, she will borrow it, and it will be good to have her. Covers turned down, and towels and wash cloths placed where she can find them, I close the door and turn out the light.

I find that the emotions of the day have simply exhausted me. I think for a minute about grabbing a couple of cookies and a glass of milk before bed but then decide against it. I am so tired. Before I forget, I put the candies I bought in a bowl outside and put a note on it to take one. I know that some kids will take more than that. Honestly, out here, we might not get more than a handful of Trick or Treaters, but anyway, hopefully, some kid won't get super greedy and take it all. Tonight, I will just have to let whatever happens to be okay. I am bushed. I head into the bathroom and brush my teeth, wash my face, and go crawl into bed. I must have fallen asleep as soon as my head hit the pillow. My mind is back at Patton Middle School. "Hey, Rodriguez boy. What do you have to do with all this? How do you fit into this story?" I ask.

"Who, me? Larry, why, don't you know? I am your people. I am those who have gone on before, and I am your future. I am your connection to the "Great Cloud of Witnesses," and I am your link to your ghost girl. Surely you know that. I think you have known that all along.

"Well, hmmm. Rodriguez. You are the key that unlocks the door to this great mystery at Patton Middle School. How can it be so simple?" Suddenly, a passage from the Old Bible comes into my mind, and I am overwhelmed with God's ways.

"The wolf also shall dwell with the lamb, and the leopard shall lie down with the kid; and the calf and the young lion and the fatling together, and a little child shall lead them."

I wake up then. Or at least that's all I remember. I look over at the clock, and it's time for me to get up. I have forgotten to set the clock. Truthfully, my body is so trained to get up early that I never really need a clock, but as a habit, I do it anyway. But last night, I guess I was just so tired I forgot. No worries. I'm up and at it, having had a bowl of oats and toast, along with a cup of coffee. I am excited for the day. It is Friday. Rosa is coming home. It is the day before Dia de los Muertos, and what I believe will be the coming together of all that has been going on at Patton. I really can't believe how clearly God made things last night, even while I rested. The little Rodriguez boy was like a huge tumbler that fell into place to help me understand why God had chosen to involve me in bringing about a resolution for our ghost girl, my own relative, and Mr. Goodland. How good to bring peace, even in realms beyond my clear comprehension.

This is All Saints Day. November 1. It is said that we all have this universal call to holiness. In order to join the saints from old and the saints of today and tomorrow, we must follow in Jesus' footsteps and conform to his image, seeking God's will in all things. Beginning my day with this understanding gives it purpose and gives me the courage to get it done. So off I go.

At Patton, I see the squad that God has brought together to bring about a good outcome for our ghost girl, and all of us go about our day, smiling or nodding to one another, but without getting started talking about what tomorrow will bring if we get going on that we all know that we won't get anything done. "Focus," I keep telling myself. The girl, her name, remember, was Rosa Maria Rodriguez. It's Rosa Maria. Though departed from this life, she is still very much alive and has been with me much of the day. It's not even creepy, but I know that she is here. How many more are here with me now, and I don't even recognize them. This is what it means to discern spiritual things, and I realize that I am just a baby in my understanding of these things.

Out on the playground, I see the little Rodriguez boy. He is playing kickball again. A kid kicks a ball out to the outfield where the Rodriguez boy catches the ball and then quickly throws the ball and gets another kid out who had left base. He is all smiles, and so are his teammates. He is quite a player and quite a kid.

"Hey, Rodriguez!" I call out to him. "Good play!"

"O, hey, Larry. Thanks. It's what we do, right?" He says and, grinning, focuses his attention back toward the game.

"Did you hear that, Rosa Maria Rodriguez? It's what we do!" She likes it too, the chill I feel down my spine tells me. "We are all one big family somehow, Rosa Maria, and tomorrow, Lord-willing, we are going to send you on to your, I mean our people, at last." The breeze around me, a tiny dust devil, maybe, or as I think, Rosa Maria, shouting her 'Yes!' to what I had to say.

The day passes, and the bell rings. All the activities of the day jump in the truck with me as I head quickly over to the bus stop to pick up Rosa and her sister, Maria. They are due in at 1600 hours, four p.m., and I have been given permission to go pick them up and come back later to finish my work. Mr. McCrank said, "You know what, Larry? Just come back in tomorrow. We are going to meet Mr. Goodland here tomorrow anyway. Just come a little early and take care of your business. Tonight, spend time with your wife.

"Yes, sir," I said. I know that it would be very hard for me to leave Rosa once I picked her up, and furthermore, it would be nearly impossible to focus on my work. Tomorrow is another day. Right now, it's all about my Rosa.

The bus station is over off Valley. I pull in just as the bus they are on comes to a stop. I knew they were due in at 1600 hours, but I honestly did not expect them to be so prompt. The bus doors open, and people start pouring out. Most look tired but are also looking around to get a feel for their surroundings. As you might guess, they just want to make sure everything is safe and as it should be. I see Rosa's sister get out of the bus. It's been a while since I've seen her, but she shares enough of my wife's DNA that I would know her anywhere. My wife, Rosa, is right behind her. My heart skips a beat. Mercy! I jump quickly out of the truck and hurry over, wrapping my arms around her, even as she is trying to see if I am there and, if so, just where I might be. Rosa! Mmmm. Welcome home, sweetheart."

"Larry, I didn't even see you." She turns and kisses me. "O, baby, it is so good to see you and be back home."

"Welcome, Maria," I say to her sister. "So glad you are here! So glad you are healthy! Que Buen Dios!"

"Absolutamente!" She responds. "How nice to see you too, Larry. Thanks for welcoming me into your home for a time."

"You are welcome, Maria. Let me get you ladies loaded up and get you home. I am sure you are both very tired from the trip."

"You got that right, Lorenzo," Rosa says. "Let's go home."

"Si, vamos a casa," I say.

It only takes a few minutes to get home from the bus stop. As we pull into the gravel driveway, the ladies share a collective sigh. "O, Larry, I can't tell you how good it is to be home and with my healthy sister. Gracias a Jesus!" Rosa says.

"Sister, your home is right in the middle of paradise," Maria says. "I love the panorama of mountains. It's like we are wrapped up in the arms of God."

Rosa and I beam. We love our home and love to have others acknowledge it as well.

"Come on in," I say to the ladies. "I'll get your luggage. Just go on in and get comfortable. I'm sure you both need to freshen up."

As I am bringing the suitcases in, Rosa appears at the door. "Honey, thanks for the beautiful red roses. You are now in the running for best husband ever! I can't believe how much God loves me! Just one blessing after another!" She said and rushed to hug my neck.

"Bingo!" I thought to myself. "It looks like I hit a home run on the flowers. Sometimes I get right."

"Now, Larry, I know you had to leave work early to pick us up. Sorry for the inconvenience. I know you have to go back to work for a while, so Maria and I will try and get us something rustled up for supper by the time you get back."

"Well, Mr. McCrank told me I could finish up tomorrow. Tomorrow we have a very important meeting at school that I am just dying to tell you about. But let me go out and get the mail and do a few things outside that need to be taken care of so that you and Maria can relax a minute before I load you down with all that has been going on here while you have been gone."

"I am very excited to hear about what you found out about the goings on at school, but you are right. We need a minute to let our hair down and get into some more comfortable clothes. I am so glad you don't have to go back in tonight. Be sure you give Mr. McCrank a big thank you for me."

I mess around outside for a few minutes, gathering the mail, mostly junk mail, as usual, and a bill from the electric company. I pick up a few small branches that blew out of the mulberry trees the other night when the wind got a little crazy on me, and a piece or two of trash that blew in with it, and then I head back in.

"So, tell us about the things that have been going on at your school. I have told Maria a little, but maybe you should start at the beginning to get us both up to speed. It sounds like you are about to bring things to a head."

"Just one thing, really quick. While I was outside, I called Lorenzo's Restaurant and ordered us a large Mesilla Valley Special Pizza. I need to run into town and pick it up in a few minutes, so don't let me forget."

"Mmm. Maria, honey. The Mesilla Valley Special Pizza is like a party in your mouth! You are going to love it!" Rosa said.

"I am pretty hungry now that you mention it," Maria said. "It sounds wonderful."

"In a few minutes, you can judge for yourself," I said. "Okay. Well, tomorrow we are going to meet with a man named Lee Goodland. Mr. Goodland, Maria, was a man that used to be the evening janitor at our school, way back when it was still called a junior high, back in the sixties and seventies. Anyway, a terrible thing happened to Mr. Goodland. Here he is, near retirement but still working to make ends meet, and the school put in these powered bleachers. We are still using them today, decades later. Anyway, it so happened that after a game one night, a little girl, say a seventh grader, but such a small thing got behind there after getting sideways with one of her friends and fell asleep. When the gym emptied, she slept right through it. So, when Mr. Goodland closed up the bleachers for the night, the poor little thing got caught in there and, unfortunately, it killed her."

"O no, Larry! That is terrible! I can't imagine how it must have made the janitor feel."

"Well, he didn't take it well. It devastated him. He couldn't handle it, and he ran away. Just disappeared. No one, not even his wife, knew where he was for the longest time. He was haunted by the event, bless his heart."

"I'd say so. O, my goodness. Poor thing. He must have blamed himself, but how could he have known?" Maria said.

"Right. Well, tomorrow we are going to meet with him. His name, as I said, is Mr. Goodland. He is living near Alamogordo now and has a caretaker. He is a very old man. Maybe he will fill us in on the details of what has become of him over the past several decades tomorrow."

"Larry, it's a tragic story, but how have you gotten involved in it now?" My wife asked.

"Remember me telling you about some strange events going on at the school before you left to be with Maria? Well, it turns out, and neither of you might believe this, and I certainly would have been very skeptical myself until recently." At this point, I paused and thought for a minute. Hmmm. There is no way you are going to believe this but let me get the whole story out before you call for the padded wagon."

They laughed at me when I said that, but I also noticed their sideways glances at one another.

"Okay. Well, here goes. Even when I came to our school, Patton Middle School, years ago, there was talk about this ghost girl that 'lived' in our school and walked our halls."

They both gave a little smile at my mention of the ghost girl.

"Right? So, anyway, there have been little tales along about cold chills and unaccounted-for noises, you know the type. No big deal. We just roll with it, and it's kind of fun. But then, this fall, these happenings started ramping up a little until this last couple of weeks; there have been multiple happenings that finally caused a few of us to realize that something had to be done. And no, we did not call Ghost Busters. So, call me crazy, but by various means, it turns out that this ghost girl is real, and she wants our help."

Now their sideways glances take a more serious turn, and I see Rosa edging over toward our home phone. She holds her hand near it and plays like she is getting ready to make the 911 call necessary to get me sized for a strait jacket. At least, I think she's playing.

"Hold on. Hear me out. I know all this is very abnormal. I don't blame you for thinking I'm crazy but hear me out on this. So, we found out that this girl wants to get things right with Mr. Goodland because she knows that he blames himself for what happened. She can't let him go to his grave thinking that. She wants to free him of his guilt. She wants to see him one last time to forgive him if that is what he needs. She has to do this in order to join the 'Great Cloud of Witnesses' the Bible talks about in Hebrews 12. You remember that verse. "We are surrounded by a great cloud of witnesses…." It turns out that the scripture is not just waxing poetic here, but that this passage is true. Those who have gone on before us are continually watching and joining us in our pilgrimage through this life. Tomorrow, we celebrate Dia de los Muertos, as you ladies know. On that day, the dead come back and, in a very special way, join us as a family again. I used to think that was quaint, but I certainly didn't really believe it, but it turns out the old people were not all crazy after all. This really happens. And on this day, the cycle is open for our school's ghost girl to go home to be with her people. She is past ready, but she has been waiting all this time to get things right with Mr. Goodland before she goes. Tomorrow, we introduce these two, allowing them to bring peace into one another's lives. The girl will be released to join her people, and if I get my guess, Mr. Goodland will be released from this life to do the same. I believe he has been living, whether he knows it or not, to find this peace before he dies."

The ladies are just staring at me. I can see Rosa make up her mind. She steps away from the phone and over to me. She hugs me and says, "Sweetheart. I had no idea. But it all sounds, in a crazy sort of way, like what you are saying could be the way it really is. I have always known, the old people have told us, plus there is just a sense we sometimes get when we are worshiping that we are not in this alone, but, wow. Wow."

"Yeah," Maria says. "Big wow."

And get ready for one more crazy thing," I say. I asked myself, why me. I asked God, 'How do I fit into this?' Through a series of events, I have been shown that, that we are also part of this cloud of witnesses. This girl is family."

"Wait. How?" Rosa says.

"I take a deep breath, and then I say her name is Rosa Maria Rodriguez."

"Well, all those names are very popular," Maria says.

"She is buried over in the Saint Joseph's cemetery off South Espina. Right beside her grave and her parents' and grandparents' graves are my own cousins and some others in our family.

"We are family, and God is using me to help one of our own to get home. I know it sounds weird, and I know that I am certainly not worthy of being involved in such a spiritual event, but for whatever reason, God has chosen me, among others, to help this girl go home." There is a pause in time. No one speaks. Then I say, "Tomorrow is the day."

"May it be so," my Rosa says.

"Yes, Larry, amen. May it be just as you have said," says Maria.

We are all joined then. We are drawn together like pieces of steel to a magnet, and we join hands. We lift our eyes up to heaven, and we sing a song that Rosa begins, but we all know by heart. This is the chorus:

Precious Lord, take my hand; Lead me on; let me stand
I am tired; I'm weak, I am worn: Through the storm, through the

night; Lead me on to the light; Take my ha-and, precious Lord Lead me home.

It seems to me that we are all joined in heart as we conclude this song. It is as if our spirits have joined together, and the spirits of those who have gone on before have joined us as well. We, none of us, have words to express just how this feels, but we look to one another, we squeeze one another's hand, and we just heave a sigh of comfort that our Lord is with us in this place.

Rosa breaks the spell of the moment and says, "Pizza! I almost forgot. What do you say we all load up in the truck and go eat it there? They have such a nice ambiance and great bread. Larry and I mix up this little paste with grated cheese and oil and sometimes red chile pepper. It's to die for!"

In a flash, we are all loaded in front of my old pick-up truck and off to Lorenzo's. What a meal!

Chapter 21

Saturday morning comes with a cool breeze and an azure blue sky. The temperature in New Mexico in early November is still relatively mild. Lows in the thirties, highs in the sixties. It really couldn't get any better than this. This morning I check the weather and find it a typical thirty-six degrees Fahrenheit, but with the breeze coming in at ten miles an hour, it is a bit chilly. I make sure to grab my navy-blue waist jacket that has a Larry patch over the left breast and LPPS over the right. I have had this La Plata Public Schools jacket for years. It is worn and frayed in spots, but I wear it like a badge of honor. There is no shame in my work and no shame in making a clear decision to earn the bread that comes to my table. My Abuela taught me to take pride in my work and never, never let the government or anyone else carry a load I could carry for myself.

My sweet wife and her sister are both still fast asleep as I leave the house this morning. That trip on a bus all the way from Chihuahua is exhausting. When I get home today, they will both be refreshed and ready to see what's what, but as for now, rest is the best option. Besides, I have much to contemplate as I head into school. What will happen today? I can't help but believe that this could be a wonderful day for all involved, but, of course, there is always that little voice of doubt. I am reminded of the man who brought his son to Jesus. The boy was possessed by a demon who continually did the boy harm. The dad, in desperation, brought his son to Jesus' disciples, but they could not cast the demon out. When Jesus came down from the Mount of Transfiguration, where he had met with Moses and Elijah and been confirmed by a voice from heaven, the man brought his son to Jesus. "Sir," the man said. "I brought my son to your disciples to have them cast out the demon that tortures my son, but they could not do it."

"Bring the boy to me," Jesus says.

"If you can do anything..." the father says.

"If I can?" Jesus says back. "All things are possible to those who believe."

Then this is the part that always gets me.

"Lord, I do believe. Help my unbelief!" The father says.

Jesus commands the demon to come out, and he does. All are amazed. The father is relieved, and his son is the normal boy he had once been.

Later, Jesus' disciples ask him privately, "Why couldn't we drive it out?"

"This kind," Jesus said, "can only be driven out by prayer and fasting."

Your Bible will have a footnote that says "fasting" was not in the original manuscripts but was added later. No matter, I skip breakfast and even the coffee that puts me into drive so many mornings. I want the Lord in on this, and I want myself to be as clear and connected to his Name and his power as I can possibly be. Lives and souls depend upon it.

As I pull into the school parking lot, it is only 0700 hours. I am two hours ahead of the meeting and am the first to arrive. I know it is crazy to come so early, but I also know that I will be super antsy if I stay at home. Who can focus on what is around them when so much lies ahead of them? Getting out of the old Ford, I feel that cool breeze working its way around the collar of my work jacket. I zip it up a little tighter and head on in. Once inside, I figure I will do a little preparation for Monday. It will make my week start easier and help keep my mind off the meeting that is soon to come. There is not really much to do, but since I left a bit early yesterday to pick up Rosa and her sister, Maria, I know I need to sweep the halls again and make sure I picked up all the trash and emptied the pencil sharpeners. I figure I will go ahead and wipe down the desks too. This time of year, kids are bound to be carrying some kind of sickness in with them to share with the crowd. Exposures like that build immunities, but I'd be lying if I said, therefore no one will get sick. If you don't get enough sleep, don't drink enough water, eat too many sweets, and leave off keeping your hands clean, well, you will most likely get sick with no one to blame but yourself. Teaching kids these basic protocols are not done consistently enough on the adult side and do not adhere to enough on the kid side. Still, one way or another, we get by for the most part.

I was down in the seventh-grade hall, just sweeping past Mr. Jackson's room, when I felt this chill come over me. "Good morning, Rosa Maria," I say. "I love your name, by the way. I suppose somehow you and I are related. I am honored if that's the case. I do hope we can work things out for you today. I know that you are very excited about the possibility of finally spending this holiday with your family. All of your family. Mr. Goodland should be here in a couple of hours. I think it's cool what you want to do for him. It says so much about you. "By their fruits, you shall know them," the Bible says. Oh, and if you hear a voice today, one that is not that horrible voice that cursed poor Mr. Goodland, but a voice calling you to come and join your family, I think that is one you will want to respond to, don't you?"

I was just talking away, just the school's ghost girl and me. Well, I was talking, and maybe she was listening. Honestly, I would not have wanted someone to walk in just then, but you know how you do when you are alone? Or at least I do. You can imagine my surprise when all the sudden I hear:

"Larry?" It was a little girl's voice. I looked all around. No one. It came again. "Larry, It's me, Rosa Maria. My mother is the only one that calls me Rosa Maria. She said she loved the way it rolled off her tongue. I have so missed her. Anyway, you can just call me Rosa."

Chills ran all over me then. I was not afraid, but this was way out of my wheelhouse. Well, I guess maybe I was afraid, but not that I would be hurt. Her voice was so sweet and kind. Just a young girl. I guess once you die, you don't age.

"Hello, Rosa." It felt really weird saying that. I mean, I know I was just talking away to this little girl, but that was before I, well, I don't know. It is just weird.

"What voice should I be listening for, Larry?" She asked.

"Voice?" I say. "Oh, O yeah, In the Bible, in the book of John, Jesus tells those who are listening that he is the good shepherd. He says that his sheep know his voice and follow him. Today, Rosa, if things work out the way we hope they do, Mr. Goodland will hear you forgive him and basically give him permission to quit carrying his guilt, and you will be free to go on to meet with your family in the celebration of Dia de los Muertos. When you leave this school, at last, bless your heart, you will hear the voice of Jesus calling you. Be sure to follow him. That other old voice of guilt and bitterness that drove poor Mr. Goodland to run away could be here too. Don't get confused. You belong to Jesus Christ. Listen to his voice only. He will tell you what you need to do."

"Wow. Do you really think so? I do believe in Jesus and placed my faith in him so many years ago. It was because of him that I have stayed all these years. He would have wanted me to make things right with Mr. Goodland. And somehow, I know that time really doesn't matter when we go to be with Jesus. We are just with him, and that is enough. Thanks for reminding me of that. I will be listening to his voice. I can't wait." She paused a minute and then said, "Larry, this is going to be the best day ever!"

I could almost see her smile. Lord knows I could feel it. This was going to be a great day. Best ever. "This is the day that the Lord has made. Let us rejoice and be glad in it," came to mind again.

It was just then that I heard someone coming in the front door. I came back around the corner to the science hall, where Mrs. Montes's classroom is, and saw Mr. McCrank coming in, shaking himself.

"Good morning, Mr. McCrank," I called out. "Cold out there?"

'Yeah. Good morning, Larry. That cool breeze just seemed to get down inside of me this morning. I was just trying to get my blood flowing a little. You sure got here early."

"Yes, sir. I woke up and knew that I would just go crazy hanging around the house, so I came on in. I have only been here a few minutes, though. You are pretty early yourself."

"I guess in that, Larry, you and I are pretty much alike. I have been looking forward to this day, and I can't wait to have it over and done. That man needs peace; our little ghost girl needs peace, and, quite frankly, we need peace too. If things go well today, we will have had a great day."

"Best day ever!" Came a child's voice.

"Mr. McCrank actually ducked, looking all around like someone had taken a shot at him.

"What?" He said. "Who was that? What's going on around here, Larry?"

"Mr. McCrank," I said, smiling, "our ghost girl has come out of her shell. Her name is Rosa. Say hello to Rosa."

"Rosa?" He said questioningly.

"Hello, Mr. McCrank," her voice replied.

It was funny watching Mr. McCrank process this in his mind. I can't help but laugh about it even now.

"How?"

"Mr. McCrank, I have been here since the day I died. I have witnessed many things. I have made my presence known in many ways, but only today have I been able to speak. I know not how," she said in a way that sounded like it ought to be in a Charles Dickens' story.

"Whoa, this is too creepy," Mr. McCrank said.

"Don't be afraid, Mr. McCrank. I won't hurt you. Today is my liberation day and my homecoming day. I am so excited about seeing Mr. Goodland. Thank you for helping get that set up."

"Rosa. Rosa, I am glad to meet you. And you are welcome. Larry and I are both very excited about helping get you together at last with your people. I have to say that I really don't understand any of this, but it's happening whether I do or not. So, let's make it great."

"Yes!" Rosa said. "The best day ever!"

About that time, Mr. Jackson came in. By now, it was after 0800 hours. He looked his usual spry and happy self, but if possible, there might have been even a bit more gleam in his eyes than usual.

"Hello, Mr. Jackson. You certainly are here early," I said.

"Hey, Jackson, what are you always so happy about?" Mr. McCrank said.

"Sir, this is the day that the Lord has made. I intend to rejoice and be glad in it," Mr. Jackson said.

"How about that?" I thought.

"Well, one thing I can say for you, Mr. Jackson, is you are the most consistent person I have ever witnessed living that out," Mr. McCrank said.

"Thank you, sir. You have just made my day. I really do like working here and feel blessed to have a chance to help these kids see a direction with purpose in their lives. Not only that but the way you and Ms. David and Mrs. Baez just let us do our job and teach without trying to recreate us in the district's image. I really appreciate that. I think everyone benefits from that mindset.

"Well said," Mrs. Douglass said, who had just come in as Mr. Jackson played his monologue. "I know that I have only been here for a few months now, and it is hard to break into a new school, but the admin here has let me create an environment in the library that I think best benefits these children. That hasn't been the case in every place I've been."

"You do a great job, both of you," Mr. McCrank said.

I have worked at this school for several years now and have known Mr. McCrank all this time, but I don't think I've felt such a positive vibe or heard so many encouraging words coming from him from the time I was hired on until now. I could easily take another dose of that.

Rosa, our ghost girl, had been quiet for a time, just listening in on our unsuspecting co-workers. I kind of thought she was about due to putting her two cents worth in, and I knew that when she did, it would be worth seeing the other's reaction. I was not disappointed.

"Mr. Jackson, can I say something?" She asked.

Now, Mr. Jackson thought it was Mrs. Douglass that spoke up. Even though it didn't sound like her voice, she was the most obvious choice for speaker. He looked at Mrs. Douglass, who was looking very confused and said, "Yes, ma'am. What can I do for you?"

It took a moment for Mrs. Douglass to get her tongue untied. "I, I am not the one that said that," she said, still looking very confused.

"Who then?" Mr. Jackson said.

"It was me. Don't be afraid, you two. It's me, Rosa. I am the school's "Ghost Girl."

Mr. Jackson looked at Mrs. Douglass and then Mr. McCrank, and myself. Mrs. Douglass did the same. And then they both started laughing. Kind of a nervous laugh.

"You guys really had us going there," Mrs. Douglass said.

"Yeah, I don't know how you did that, but creepy," Mr. Jackson said.

"It is kind of creepy," Rosa's voice again. I don't mean to be scary, but I do want to talk to you all and get to know you better before I leave," she said.

Now all this was happening in the hallway, so sort of in unison, we all just started walking into Mr. Jackson's classroom and plopped down. This was making our knees weak.

Mr. McCrank said, "Okay, Rosa. You know everyone here. We know something about you, and we hope that today we can resolve a long-held problem of yours."

I spoke up and said, "Yeah, Rosa, we all want for you to finally get to go home. Mr. Goodland will be here soon, but before he gets here, will you explain a couple of things to us?"

"Sure, Larry. What do you want to know?"

Can you explain that deal in Mrs. Montes' classroom? What was that all about? I know you said you didn't want to scare us, but that was scary."

"Yeah. I'd say," Mr. McCrank again. "What was with the loud noise and the transistor radio and the flying papers?"

"Hmmm, sorry about that. I guess I was having a tantrum. I am only thirteen years old, you know. I was trying to figure out how to get out of here. I thought, I don't know, science. Science is supposed to be the search for truth, or so I remember hearing somewhere. So, I was looking for answers in the books and papers. When I found that radio, it was behind an access panel; by the way, who knows why? I suddenly knew what I had to do. I had to find Mr. Goodland and help him find his peace and let go of his guilt."

"Wait," Mr. McCrank said. "What did that radio have to do with anything?"

"That radio was Mr. Goodland's. He used to play that radio when he was cleaning up at night. When I saw it, I realized that if I could find him and get things cleared up with him once and for all, both he and I could find our peace."

"Okay. I have one for you," said Mrs. Douglass, looking around like she was trying to find Rosa.

"That's fine, Mrs. Douglass. And I want to thank you for helping me. I didn't mean to scare you, but you were the only woman here that I seemed to have a connection with. Now don't get me wrong. I love Ms. David, but she is so busy keeping this school running, loving on these kids, and showing them that going to school where respecting others is a good thing. I just couldn't bring myself to add to her load. But you were new, and you seemed like you really cared so...."

"Thank you, Rosa. I am honored. I am glad to help in any way I can. But I don't understand the poetry books. Was that you?"

Things were quiet for a minute, and then Mr. Jackson said, "I don't think she heard you, Mrs. Douglass. Try your question again."

"No. I heard her," Rosa said. "I," there was a sigh. "I just never was very good with language arts, Mr. Jackson. I remembered that our teacher, her name was Mrs. Pollard, would read us these poems about people dying or that were dead. I don't know why. She seemed so sad most of the time. Maybe someone she loved, her husband or child or friend or something, had died, and she hadn't gotten over it. We used to talk about it among ourselves, us kids, but none of us had the nerve to ask her. We did like her. I remember that. And the poems she read made me feel sad too, or maybe the right word is melancholy. Anyway, when she would read that poem by Edgar Alan Poe, I think he was her favorite. I would just get chills listening to it. I thought maybe if I could find that poem and, I don't know, study it somehow, maybe I could find out how to get out of here and back to that Crowd of Witnesses that I heard Mr. Jackson and Larry talking about."

"Cloud of Witnesses," Mr. Jackson corrected. "Rosa, the Bible says in Hebrews that only together with us can they receive that which is promised. That's at the end of chapter eleven. One day Jesus will come back to this earth. The trumpet of God will sound, the clouds will be rolled back like in a great thunderstorm, and Jesus will appear with all the hosts of heaven. Imagine that, Rosa. Angels by the thousands, by the tens and hundreds of thousands with Jesus right in the middle, and every eye will see them. This will not be a secret mission.

It will be a universal announcement. The time has come. All those who have died, including you and all your family that have preceded you, will rise up from your graves to meet Jesus in the air, and those of us who are still alive will join you. It will be the greatest reunion ever and a celebration like no other. There will be a judgment then. Everyone will be judged according to what they have done, whether good or bad. Those who have put their trust in Christ will have him as their advocate, someone who stands with them. It will be like when we stand before the judgment seat of God that Jesus will be our stand in. He has already paid the price of all sins. And all those who put their trust in him will never be put to shame. He will say to the Father something like, "This one's with me. I've paid for his sins, and he or she, whatever the case may be, has accepted the gift of my sacrifice." Then a voice will come back saying, "Well done, good and faithful servant, enter into your master's inheritance, for I was hungry, and you gave me something to eat, I was thirsty, and you gave me something to drink, I was a stranger, and you welcomed me, I was naked, and you clothed me, I was sick and in prison, and you visited me."

And then the people who have been saved and invited in will say, "When did we see you hungry and feed you, or thirsty and give you something to drink? When did we see you, a stranger, and invite you in or naked and clothe you? When did we see you sick and in prison and visit you?"

And then he will say, "In as much as you did it for one of the least of these my brethren, you did it to me."

And then to those who are cast out, he will say, "Depart from me you who are accursed. Depart into the eternal fire prepared for the devil and his angels because I was hungry and you gave me nothing to eat, I was thirsty, and you gave me nothing to drink, I was a stranger, and you did not invite me in, I was naked, and you didn't clothe me, I was sick and in prison, and you did not visit me?"

"When?" They will say. "We don't remember seeing you hungry or thirsty or a stranger or naked or sick or in prison. When did we fail to do those things?"

He will reply, "In as much as you did it not for one of the least of these my brethren, you did it not to me."

"Rosa, what you are doing for Mr. Goodland, although a bit unusual, is exactly what Mr. Jackson is talking about," Mrs. Douglass said, breaking into the conversation. At this point, no one thought it strange that we were apparently talking to the air.

"That's right, Rosa," I spoke up. I couldn't believe that we were having this conversation, but I wanted Rosa to know that she was absolutely doing the right thing.

"Thanks, everybody. That makes me even more excited about Mr. Goodland coming today. Anyway, Mrs. Douglass, I thought that maybe I could find the answers in that poem or in that Hamlet play that William Shakespeare wrote. I guess I was drawing at straws.

"No, Rosa. Your actions show what a strong character you have, even at age thirteen. You were in a situation that needed a solution, and you were working hard to make that happen. I am glad you heard Mr. Jackson and Mr. Rodriguez talking. So that was the thing that helped you know what you needed to do?" Mr. McCrank said. We were all looking at Mr. McCrank with a deeper respect for him than we had ever had. This man, who we had all come to respect, was showing us that there was much to admire about him as well.

"Yes, sir. I knew that if somehow, I could get a hold of Mr. Goodland and make him see that my death was not his fault and give him peace, then, well, maybe somehow that would allow me to join my family and be at peace. also."

"Well, I'd say you are one smart little girl, Rosa. Mrs. Douglass said. "I am still curious, though. Which Poe poem were you looking for? He wrote several dark and troubling poems. He had a lot of grief in his own life, I think."

"Yes, ma'am. That's what Mrs. Pollard said. We read a poem about a couple who were very much in love, and then she got sick and died. The man was so grief-stricken that he would go out to her in the tombs every night and lay down so he could sleep by her side. What I wanted to do was be with my people, so...."

"Annabelle Lee. That's the name of the poem. It is a sad one, alright. And you are right. He did go out to her, night after night, to sleep at her sepulcher. Too sad for me. I am sorry that you have felt that level of grief at such a young age. Today. Today might just be the day when all that sadness ends for you."

Mrs. Douglass had just finished speaking when the front door opened, and there was Mr. Goodland and his caretaker, John. In the morning sun that shone behind them through the front doors, there appeared to be the brightness of angels all around them. Maybe it was real, I don't know, but it certainly was cool and made for a grand entrance.

I went quickly to the door to greet them. The others were with me, but I took the lead. I had work in common in life to make the connection with Mr. Goodland, and I felt that I needed to be the one to bring him in.

"Mr. Goodland, thank you for coming. What do you think? How does the old school look?" I asked.

He was quiet for a moment. His eyes were surveying everything around him. Finally, he said, "Wow. The outsides have changed with the chain-link fence and the portables and picnic tables in the common area, but inside, it looks a lot the same, at least in the entrance and down this hallway. I thought it would be hard to come back, and it is in a way, but in another way, I have missed these old halls. They were home to me for a while. They became part of me. Does that make sense, or am I just an old man talking out of his head?"

"It makes perfect sense. This place is my domain, and I try to take care of it like it was my own. I get what you're saying." I sort of adjusted myself around and pointed to the others who were with me. "Mr. Goodland, this is Mr. McCrank, one of our vice-principals. And this is Mr. Jackson, one of our seventh-grade teachers, and this is Mrs. Douglass, our librarian."

All of the others nodded or waved with "Pleased to meet you," and We're glad you are here."

Mr. Goodland, will you come with us down to Mr. Jackson's room. We feel like this would be a good place for us to meet," Mr. McCrank said.

Mr. Goodland nodded his head and said, "Lead on, sir. I've been looking forward to this day."

I wondered in what way he had been looking forward, with trepidation or anticipation of deliverance. No matter, he was here, and the hoped-for resolution was at hand. I just knew that, somehow.

We all filed into Mr. Jackson's room and took seats at the students' desks. Mr. Goodland remained in his wheelchair with his caretaker standing behind him.

Mr. Jackson went to the front of the room and explained why we were in his room and what we hoped to accomplish today. It kind of felt like a regular day at school. Kind of.

"Welcome to my classroom. This room is called "The Chapel" because of the arch in the middle that reminds some people of a church building. I love this room and certainly feel like God is here with me every day. Indeed, I believe his presence is here with us right now. But Mr. Goodland, there is someone else here with us right now that we have not yet introduced you to."

Mr. Goodland looked around, trying to identify someone that he had somehow missed earlier.

"Rosa Maria Rodriguez, would you introduce yourself, please?" Mr. Jackson asked.

"Hello, Mr. Goodland, it's me, Rosa."

You could see Mr. Goodland's visible flinch. Ducking his head, he pivoted it around, searching for the source of the voice. His caretaker did the same, a look of terror on his face.

"Who said that? What's this about? What's going on here?" Mr. Goodland was almost ready to run, it seemed.

"Mr. Goodland, it's me, Rosa. You don't know my name, but maybe you remember my voice. It's been a long time, Mr. Goodland."

"Are…are you the little girl from behind the bleachers? But how can that be? How am I talking to you?" He asked.

"Mr. Goodland, I am so glad you are here. I am the one that died that night O so long ago. But it was totally not your fault. You didn't know that I was there. I shouldn't have been. I had fallen asleep back there, Mr. Goodland. It was just something that happened."

I didn't mean for that to happen, Rosa. I am so sorry," Mr. Goodland sobbed back.

"I know, I know. You worked so hard to get me out and then to try to save my life. I saw everything, Mr. Goodland. It is hard to explain, but as my spirit was leaving my body, I was still there, watching you make the call to your wife, watching you beg the paramedics to help me. I know how distraught you were, and I also heard that Voice that was shouting at you, telling you that you were guilty. He caused you to get in your truck and drive away before I could make it clear to you that you were not at fault and that I blamed you for nothing. I had lived a good life with my mother and father and brother and sisters. I had been a happy girl, for the most part. I loved school and my family, though we didn't have much. Like you, I think, Mr. Goodland. Our happiness was not dependent upon how much we had but on enjoying and being thankful for what we had. When I died, you didn't take that away from me but gave me the opportunity to dwell deeply on what was important in my life and understand how blessed I was. There was a girl I had gone to the ball game with who met another friend and ditched me that night. My feelings were hurt, and I went off by myself. I wandered into the school house and the library and found a book to read that I really got into. It made me realize that there were others like me, growing up and doing the best they could. I wasn't even upset with my friend, who ditched me after a while. It was okay. She was just a kid, like me, that was being taught life lessons, little by little. I bet she grew up to be a good person. It just takes some rounding to happen in our lives in order for us to become what we need to be. So, Mr. Goodland, I wanted you to come today so that you could hear me forgive you for anything you have felt guilty about concerning what happened to me and tell you it was not your fault. I want you to have peace, Mr. Goodland. Have peace and rest. God showed me that in order for me to have peace, I needed to help you find your peace."

"Wow," Mr. McCrank said. "I guess when you aren't able to speak out for several decades, it takes a while to get your feelings out. Good job, little lady, and very wise words from one so young as you."

Mr. McCrank was right, of course, but it was just blithering compared to what happened next.

Bit by bit, Rosa Maria Rodriguez began to appear. Her manifestation took a minute, but there she was, all five feet of her. She smiled at all of us and walked over to Mr. Goodland, and took his hands. They looked at one another for the longest time, and then she reached over and hugged his neck, kissing him on the forehead. "Be at peace, Mr. Goodland."

Tears streamed down Mr. Goodland's cheeks. Rosa leaned back from him, still holding his hands. Again looking one another in the eyes, we began to see Rosa fade away. "I am going now. Thanks to all of you who showed me how to find peace and especially for bringing Mr. Goodland to me. My family is calling me. And Mr. Jackson, you are going to love this part. There he is with his shepherd's crook." She was looking very intently toward the east, which was just up the hall toward the front of the school. "I'm coming, Jesus!" She sighed, and tears were streaming down her eyes. I didn't know that spirits could cry but truthfully, I don't seem to know hardly anything about what goes on in the spirit world. It is that world of the Great Cloud of Witnesses.

And her presence just left us. She was gone at peace at last. No experience in my life will ever match that one.

I looked around, and everyone was crying. Some with just tears streaming, and Mr. Jackson, honestly, sobbing. It was over. The peace that came to Rosa on this Dia de los Muertos had come to Mr. Goodland as well. There was a glow about him, much like what we saw behind him as he came into our building, but this time it was not sunshine that illuminated him. It was like the presence of the Spirit of God was on him. Maybe this is what the scripture meant when it referred to "tongues of fire."

"I'm going home now. Thank you, Larry. Thank you, everybody. I can now live out whatever days God gives me in peace. John, let's go home." His caretaker began to roll him out of Mr. Jackson's classroom door, and all of us followed behind. Suddenly I remember the radio.

"Hold on a minute, Mr. Goodland. I think I have something that belongs to you. I ran down the hall quickly to my janitor's closet. Everybody else just watched me dash away, and then I was back in a flash. Holding the radio out to him, I said, "How about this? Does this look familiar?"

Mr. Goodland took it in his hands, and then a look of recognition came on his face. "Why, it's my old radio. Where in the world did this come from?"

"Not really sure where you left it, Mr. Goodland, but our ghost girl found it in her effort to find you, and I think she would want you to have it back," I said.

"Hmm," he said, shaking his head. "Very well, then. Thank you." John moved him forward and, in a moment, with goodbyes all around; they were out the door. Just as they went out, a car pulled quickly into the parking lot. It stopped so quickly that the tires squealed. A lady jumped out of the car and ran around to the passenger side, where she opened the door for an old lady. Very slowly, she exited the car and stood up, looking back at the school. All of us walked toward the entrance to witness the scene.

"Lee Goodland, Is that you?" The old woman said. A look of recognition came on Mr. Goodland's face.

"Juanita? Juanita, honey, is that you?"

How God pulled this reunion off, we did not know, nor did we interfere with this reunion to find out. It is sufficient to say that God once again was on the move.

Breaking ourselves away from the scene and with eyes full of wonder, Mr. McCrank spoke to us. "Good work, everybody. I feel like we did good today." There was a musing among us that we all seemed to savor, and then, after a time, he said, "Well, what do you say we all go home?" It sure seems like our work is done here for today."

"Here, here," said Mrs. Douglass. And then she surprised us all by quoting the last of Martin Luther King jr.'s "I Have a Dream" speech.

"Free at last. Free at last. Thank God Almighty, we are free at last!"

Epilogue

My name is Larry Rodriguez. I am a school janitor at Patton Middle School. I am not a detective or a ghostbuster, but I have been a witness to some strange things here at our school. The scripture says, "We walk by faith, and not by sight." It is in this faith that I believe that Rosa Maria Rodriguez, alias "Ghost Girl," who has long wandered the halls of Patton, has now gone on to be with her family on this Dia de los Muertos. Somehow, God chose my co-workers and me here at the school, all of us so very different, to form a rescue squad to help Rosa join that Great Cloud of Witnesses that I have long read about but just recently begun to comprehend. Hebrews 11 is a chapter of biblical heroes who lived their lives in faith, looking forward to the coming of the Messiah and God's presence coming to dwell among us. Then verses 39 and 40 read like this: "Yet all these, though they were commended for their faith, did not receive what was promised, since God had provided something better so that they would not, apart from us, be made perfect." *New Revised Standard Bible*

Those that have died and have gone on ahead of us, including Rosa Maria Rodriguez, my distant relative by blood and my sister in Christ, have gone on from here ahead of us. She is still very much alive and well celebrated by her family at her coming, they are standing watch over us. Waiting. For me. And for you. And for all who seek his appearing. "Amen. Come, Lord Jesus!"

www.ingramcontent.com/pod-product-compliance
Lightning Source LLC
Chambersburg PA
CBHW070642120526
44590CB00013BA/830